REBELLION

**Saskatchewan Uprising of 1885,
The only Armed Rebellion in
Canadian History, led by
Louis Riel: Hero or Traitor?**

Stan Modrak

Branden Books, Boston

© Copyright 2013
By Branden Books

Library of Congress Cataloging-in-Publication Data

Modrak, Stan.
Rebellion : Saskatchewan uprising of 1885--the only armed
rebellion in Canadian history, led by Louis Riel : hero or traitor? /
by Stan Modrak.
pages cm
Includes bibliographical references and index.
ISBN 978-0-8283-2505-9 (pbk. : alk. paper)
1. Riel, Louis, 1844-1885.
2. Dumont, Gabriel, 1838-1906.
3. Riel Rebellion, 1885.
4. Revolutionaries--Canada--Biography.
5. Métis--Prairie Provinces--Biography.
I. Title.

F1060.9.R53M63 2013
971.05'4--dc23
          2013038003

Paperback ISBN 9780828325059 $15.95
E-Book ISBN 9780828325066 $9.99

Branden Books
PO Box 812094
Wellesley MA 02482
www.brandenbooks.com

TABLE OF CONTENTS

PREFACE

First, here's a little background history on Canada's peoples, weather resources and government. The Inuit and the Indian Nations were the first to populate Canada's arctic north, forests and prairies. Leif Eriksson, the Norse explorer is believed to be the first European to reach the shores of Canada arriving at the coast of Labrador or Nova Scotia in 1000 B.C.

European settlement did not begin to take place until the 1500's. Later, about 1534, Jacques Cartier, a French explorer, discovered the St. Lawrence River. His intrepid Frenchmen were searching the possibility of furs and shortly thereafter planted the French *Fleur de Lys* claiming Canada for his countrymen. Starting in 1541 French settlers began to arrive, but no official national settlement was established until the year 1604. The first settlement took foothold on Nova Scotia naming their settlement Port Royal.

The original settlement that they colonized as "New France" was in 1608 Quebec. This nascent colony numbered only about 300 adventuresome Frenchmen. A leader, Samuel Champlain began an arduous campaign to promote and turn his new world into a thriving, self-supporting colony. In the year 1609 and for ensuing decades New France was primarily a trading post and embassy. Their tiny colony was situated on the brim of a new and unexplored country dominated by native Indian tribes speaking many diverse languages. Indian names like Cree, Western Cree, Blackfoot, Assiniboia, Ojibwa and others were to dot the landscape.

In 1628 the French King dispatched 400 hopeful, new settlers to Quebec. Upon their sailing from the shores of France war broke out between England and France, and they immediately returned. David Kirk, an English Naval Commander blockaded the St. Lawrence River.

A burgeoning French colonial growth showed a steady increase in the 1630's. The King of France ruled his "New France" from 1663 to 1763. A company of English fur traders staked a claim into Hudson Bay and were chartered in 1670. This gave the company, which became known as the Hudson's Bay Company enormous commercial entry and access to the Canadian wilderness and its tremendous fur potential. At this time also, English and French hunters, trappers and fur traders not only began to populate the Canadian spacious Northwest Territory but soon they additionally began to intermarry native Indian women. The Metis, or mixed bloods are the principle players in the 1885 rebellion.

In 1689 the French and Indian wars began a new Canadian phase as England and France once again declared war. After eight years, the French and English made peace. Soon afterwards the warring, deadly Iroquois made peace also. Four years later, in 1701, the Iroquois Five Nations war chiefs declared their neutrality in France and England's colonial warring. In 1713 all of French Newfoundland was ceded to their English opponents. Additionally, French forces withdrew from their forts on Hudson Bay, reluctantly accepting England's title to the Bay.

Population along the St. Lawrence River began to resume its rapid growth. The population in 1700 had doubled to thirty five thousand into the 1730's. Again they doubled by the 1750's. Then in 1744, war! Again France and England resumed their Canadian struggles. The French colonists were then deported to France. This signaled the end of Frances' military power and influence on the Atlantic coast. Then came 1756 and the formal onset of the "Seven Years War." The French leaders named Louis Joseph Montcalm as military commander of all continental French forces.

In addition to the French, the English also began exploring the hinterlands of Canada for its fur and fishing trade. After a conflict with French forces in 1713, England won control of Newfoundland, Nova Scotia and Hudson Bay. The Seven Years War began in 1756 enabled England to gain increased control of the country. In 1763 the Treaty of Paris gave England full control of Canada.

At the end of the Seven Years War, more than twenty thousand of Britain's one hundred and forty thousand- man army were ensconced in North America. After the loss of Fort Duquesne on the Ohio River and the destruction of Fort Frontenac at Lake Ontario, French military control was weakened considerably. Heading the British army against the French leader Montcalm, General Thomas Wolfe took command. By the night of Sept. 12-13, 1759, Wolf's army seized a path up the western cliffs of Quebec leading to the Plains of Abraham. By morning Wolfe had four thousand infantry and deadly artillery prepared on the Plains of Abraham. Numerically, both Wolfe's and Montcalm's forces ready for battle were pretty much equal in strength. However, as the conflict erupted, deadly, close-range volleys of Wolfe's skilled and accurate artillery tore the French lines apart causing tremendous casualties. Sometime into the action England's General Wolfe died on the battlefield. The French General Montcalm, grievously wounded during the retreat, also died the next day. Now Quebec, the Capitol of New France was forced to yield to the British forces.

New settlers began to spread across the land by 1760 and 1840. The Metis, hunters, trappers and fur traders formed a distinctive ethnic people. Primarily French, with some English, intermarried with native Indians. Assiniboine and the Western Cree were the main occupants of the territory that is today southern Manitoba and Saskatchewan Provinces. Colonists increased again 16-fold by 1841. In North America there were now over 1.5 million people that were non-aboriginal. This rapid influx of new settlers resulted in the Native people being outnumbered almost 10 to 1. Lt. Governor Simcoe, admiring the agriculture abilities and experience of American pioneers, encouraged American settlers from New York and Pennsylvania to enhance the colonies population. In Upper Canada race mixing of Scots and Irish settlers was common after 1815.

In the booming fur trade, St. Lawrence and Hudson Bay interests sought trade advantages over three decades. By the year 1825 the Hudson Bay monopoly operated 45 trading posts. The area's Cree and Assiniboine natives had to find other ways to remain as the primary suppliers of European fur traders. The new timber trade soon became a considerable stimulus to continuing growth and to investments in the growing colonies. The lengthy Red River, flowing north/south from Lake Superior and into Minnesota, would eventually become the Provincial boundary between Manitoba and Saskatchewan. In 1840 there were 2,500 Metis peoples at Red River with their capitol of Pembina, just below the American border of Minnesota. Spread across seven growing colonies the population of British North America was now about 1.5 million. The chartered territory of the Hudson's Bay Company lay to the northwest of Lake Superior. In 1836 the first Canadian railway, covering only 14 miles and operating from spring to autumn was completed.. At this time in Canada's growing history, the Hudson's Bay Company's vast area of influence was known as Rupert's Land, named after a previous prominent settler. Rupert's Land comprised three-fourths of Canada's provincial and colonial domain. During 1817 and 1818 the Great Lakes were disarmed and the 49th parallel established as the boundary between Canada and the U.S.

In the years following the Treaty of Paris, English-speaking colonists surged into Canada from England and the United States. England, at this time gave Canada the right to self-government and officially established the country of Canada in 1867. The country was now made up of Upper Canada which was the area that would become Quebec and Lower Canada area that would become Ontario; Nova Scotia and New Brunswick. By 1867 the Dominion of Canada was comprised of four Provinces: Ontario, Quebec, Nova Scotia and New Brunswick. Sir John Macdonald became Prime Minister.

Canada continued its growth pattern in1869 when it bought land from the Hudson's Bay Co. later the land was divided into several provinces, one of which became Manitoba. It joined Canada in 1870 followed by British Columbia in 1871 and Prince Edward Island in 1873. Continuing to grow, in 1901 Alberta and Saskatchewan joined Canada. The country remained this way until 1949 when Newfoundland became Canada's tenth province.

Due to a long and sporadic history of conflict between England and France in Canada, division between the two is still common today in the country's languages. The official language in Quebec at the provincial level is French, and additionally there have been several initiatives promulgated by the French to insure that their language remains prominent there. Also, there have been numerous initiatives by the French for a complete secession. The year 1905 was the most recent effort for this change but it failed by only 1.2%! In other areas of Canada there are additional French-speaking communities, mostly on Canada's east coast. The majority of the rest of the country speaks English. At the federal level however, Canada is officially bilingual.

Canada is a constitutional monarchy with a parliamentary democracy and federation. There are three branches of government. The executive is the first, consisting of the head of state, who is represented by a governor general, and the prime minister, the titular head of government. The second branch is the legislative as a bicameral parliament consisting of the Senate and the House of Commons. The third branch of the government is the Supreme Court.

Industrial activity and land uses vary from region to region. The most industrialized portion of the country is in the eastern areas. However, British Columbia, Vancouver, a major seaport and Calgary are highly industrialized as well. Alberta produces 75% of Canada's oil and has an important role in the production of coal and natural gas industries.

As to Canada's topography and geography, much of its topography consists of gently rolling hills dotted with rocky outcrops, as the Canadian Shield, an ancient region contains some the world's oldest rock formations, covering about half of the landscape. The Shield's southern portion was covered with boreal forests, but the northern area is prominently tundra, being too far north to produce trees and forests. West of the Canadian Shield appear the central plains or prairies. The southern prairies are mostly grass-covered with the north portion forested. This area is also dotted with hundreds of lakes of all sizes due to land depressions cause by the last period of glaciation. To the far west the rugged Cordillera rises, emanating from the Yukon Territory into British Columbia and Alberta Provinces. Generally speaking, Canada's overall climate varies by location, but the country is classified as being temperate in the southern regions to Arctic in the harsh north. Usually the Canadian winters are long and hard in most of the country.

Due to Canada's harsh, northerly climatic conditions, about 90% of the Canadian population lives within 99 miles of the United States border. The primary reason is because of the expense of building on permafrost in the north. As to transportation, the country's Trans-Canada Highway is the longest highway in the world, stretching across the landscape for 4,725 miles (7,604 km). Resources are varied and many; nickel, zinc, potash, sulfur, asbestos, aluminum and copper. Hydro-electric power, pulp and paper, ranching and agriculture are significant to the economy.

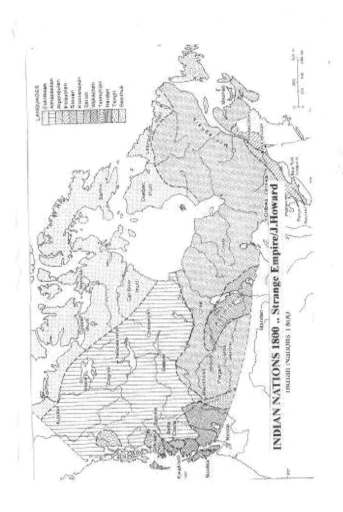

INDIAN NATIONS 1800 .. Strange Empire/J.Howard

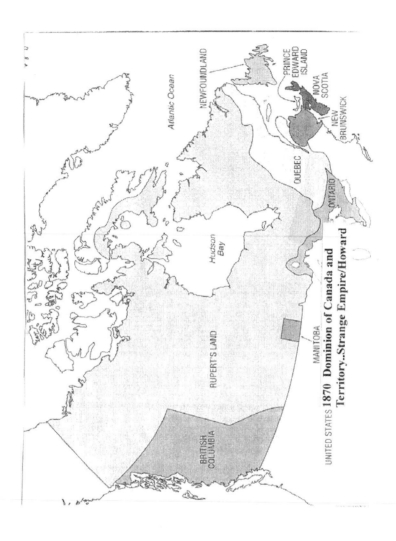

UNITED STATES 1870 **Dominion of Canada and Territory...Strange Empire/Howard**

Chapter 1
THE METIS PEOPLE

The 1885 rebellion had its roots with a sect of Canadian half-breeds known as Metis, meaning mixed blood. Referred to as half-breeds by the rest of the population, the Metis were the result of French and some English fur traders intermarrying with native Indian woman. There was also some Scottish blood in the overall mix. The Metis, speaking a mixed dialect of French and Indian, were primarily hunters, trappers and fur traders. Their daily income especially depended on the fur trade. After generations of backwoods existence the Metis developed a fiercely independent spirit.

Their language, 'Michif', consists of a mixture of French, Cree, Ojibwa and Assiniboine. Their ancestral lands covered Manitoba, Saskatchewan, Alberta and the Northwest Territories. This proud and self-sufficient people became the most experienced and prolific fur traders of colonized North America. They established settlements deep within the Canadian forested wilderness .As the French intermarried, the proportion of Indian blood in the children gradually lessened, and the term half-breed became replaced by the French Metis, or mixed-blood.

Even though the Metis peoples were of historic importance in Canada, the federal government almost immediately embarked on a campaign to assimilate and suppress them. Following their rebellion, Manitoba was created as a Canadian Province. The 1879 'Manitoba Act' gave the Metis a land grant of 1.4 million acres. But, less than half of the territory was actually ceded to them, leading to frustration and antipathy to federal government and its credibility.

The native denizens of the west in the 1700's were mostly the Sioux, Cree, Blackfoot and Assiniboine Indians and their 'relatives' by intermarriage, the Metis. The Americans and English coming into Canada never were able to win the respect or affection of the natives – they gave it freely to the French. The tribute of fear and respect was given only grudgingly to the English.

Canada was evolving from the past. Borne of violence, some despair, some hope in people's heart, it rose to a brief modicum of expected glory and tranquility in the souls and hopeful dreams of two great men to come on the scene, Louis Riel and Gabriel Dumont. In the late 1870's there was little hope of promoting any independence from the government in Ottawa. They had to be merely satisfied to achieve self-sufficiency within the British Empire.

The Metis were an illiterate, primitive society, not white. During competition for the valuable fur trade in the first half of the 19th century and for two or three decades later, the Metis frontier people dominated the rivers and prairies. They originated a system of freight transport for the prairies, establishing a new industry. Their intimate and experienced knowledge of the country – much being instinctive and inexplicable to the whites, made them indispensable. Also, most of the native Indians welcomed them as relatives and friends. Louis Riel, who was to become their leader and spokesman, believed the old values, decades old, to be good and proper for his people's successful growth.

They the Metis were often a disturbed and restive people with eastern incursions into 'their' land becoming more and more common. These incursions led to the appearance of surveyors, intent on developing and occupying increasing amounts of Metis territory. Disgruntled Metis threatened them with violence if increased land surveys were carried out. In fact, a young Riel, in his early twenties, led the first opposition and confrontation to surveying parties with sixteen unarmed followers that resulted in the surveying party backing down and leaving.

Until these incursions into their land, the Metis had never before been concerned or worried about "ownership" of the land or country, which was a concept completely foreign both to the Metis people and the Indian Five Nations.

At this time the Metis hunters, trappers and fur traders dominated the west's prairies and rivers. Boat captains and the most trustworthy and experienced guides, hunters, trappers and fur providers became visible on all waterways. Most of the native Indians made the Metis welcome after decades of intermarriage, in many cases as friends and relatives which they were.

Hardy, blessed with superior endurance in the wilds enabled the Metis to travel fifty to sixty miles a day on foot or on dogsled. In the typically snowy and icy habitat, even thirty miles on snowshoes.

French was the official language used for their letters and documents and was also favored over English for normal daily communication between each other. Louis Riel once said: "It is true that our savage origin is humble. But it is just that we honor mothers as well as our fathers. Why should we concern our-selves about what degree of mixture that we possess of Indian or European blood? Should we not be proud to say, we are Metis?"

In the 1780's the Metis from the north of the St. Lawrence River established a village they called Pembina, which translated means 'sanctified bread'. Pembina was also a Cree and Chippewa term for high-bush cranberry, nearby at the time. They were used in pemmican and when prepared, enhanced the taste. The pemmican when prepared was usually blessed by the local priest. They settled along the Red River, the major north/south River at Pembina. Red River would eventually become the boundary between Manitoba and Saskatchewan Provinces. The village of Pembina was actually just below the 49th Parallel which would later become the border between the United States and Canada.

Pembina, just a log-cabin village, became the first capitol of the new race, the Metis, (then they were known as the Red River half-breeds). Pembina also became the favorite point of assembly and planning for the annual big buffalo hunt. At the same time, Pembina also became the prairie home of the Hudson's Bay Company until 1883, when it was relocated to Fort Garry, later to become the city of Winnipeg. The Red River provided a linkage where two frontiers, two political systems merged. Pembina was a vibrant and extremely diverse center for many cultures: American, French, British, Swiss, Indian and Metis. The two main religions among the settlers were Catholic and Presbyterian.

The idea of boundaries between countries or even provinces was difficult for the Indians or the Metis peoples to pay attention to. This attitude caused a lot of governmental problems, as they wouldn't, or couldn't provide proof of citizenship. Another constant problem for government representatives was that if a half-breed was born during a buffalo hunt which might occur in the United States or in Canada, their hunts often strayed into either country.

By 1884, with the huge buffalo herds pretty much gone, there was hunger and unrest at Pembina and the Saskatchewan Territory. This led to the French and English Metis to combine forces to bring back Louis Riel from Montana in the summer of 1884, where he had been living and teaching during the five year banishment by the Canadian Government. The village of Pembina exists today as a tiny, sleepy border village in Minnesota, U.S.A.

As an inhabited village in 1780, it is the oldest community in the American northwest. This was the Nation of the Metis people. A song called them, "bois-brules", or people with skin like scorched wood. The Red River Valley was one of the most fertile regions in the world. The local people would refer to it however, as a desert to hopefully dissuade immigrants.

At the time the land and property system in place on the Red River was French originated. It enabled each settler to have a small river frontage with water rights and a "hay privilege" encompassing two miles into the prairie. Losing this 'right' would lead to conflict, frustration and unrest when the Metis resettled to Fort Garry in Manitoba. They resettled in Fort Garry when they realized in that Pembina was indeed on the United States side of the border.

In 1879 Canada, the Metis "world" was thought to be by studied estimates to be thirty three thousand people in the United States and the Canadian Northwest Territory. Metis discontent and grievances against the Dominion's Government was driven by economics and politics by their unhappy leaders. As an example of their gradual discontent Riel once composed a four-page letter in English to the Canadian Government stating that the Metis were poor, discriminated against and unhappy with their treatment under Canadian rule. Ottawa did nothing about their concerns, further frustrating and disturbing Riel and other Metis leaders

With land and rights problems occurring, the Metis needed a statesman and leader to represent their cause. This led to a young Louis Riel selected and becoming a respected leader and spokesman for the Metis cause. Especially in that the Metis had good reason to believe that the ever-intrusive eastern Government meant to interfere with their way of life, even subjugate them. Now in the Fort Garry area, the virulent seeds of the upcoming rebellion were to ultimately bear a very disruptive fruit.

It became a major disturbing element for the Metis in the Fort Garry area in that they no longer had the benefit of the old "river-lot" principle. It was too awkward for the government to ad-minister and was generally discouraged. But neither the land claims nor the river-lot principle seemed at all a minor issue to the Metis. Both were central to their way of life.

Without agreeable and effective representation in Ottawa, Their only resort was memos, letters and petitions. The Department of the Interior was consistently slow to respond, slower to act, leaving the Metis feeling much as they had a decade and a half before at Red River; a beleaguered, ignored and still vulnerable people.

Other substantial grievances remained, ones which the Canadian Government could do very little about. The old life of the Metis as carriers and freighters for the Hudson's Bay Company was mostly gone now that there were steamboats on the Saskat-chewan River and the new Canadian Pacific Railway beginning to spread westward. With the buffalo gone, the Metis took ill to the farming lifestyle. This led to hunger and to a restive people in the Saskatchewan territory by 1884.

The Metis plains and prairie hunter was partial to a garb consisting of buckskin shirts with a bright beaded design, usually in floral figures of the Cree Indians. Black woolen trousers, bound below the knee with beaded garters or ornamental leggings of wool or buckskin. A hand-woven sash was bound around the sash and looped over one shoulder. Tobacco pouch, powder bag and other articles were tied to the sash or under it. It time they adopted a round-crown felt hat of the Stetson type, usually black with a bright feather cockade or beaded band. Hunters and their women were all shod in moccasins. Their staple food of pemmican could be kept for years and proved over time to be very nutritious. A pound of pemmican was equal in food value to four pounds of fresh meat.

In the spring of 1870, thirty or forty Metis families set out from Red river on a hunt from which they didn't intend to return. Their Provisional Government still ruled at Fort Garry but it had submitted to Canadian authority. The Metis way of life and assured independence in Manitoba was finished. There were grassy, well-watered valleys in the west. Most chose a location on the South Saskatchewan River between the present cities of Saskatoon and Prince Albert. Where they finally settled they called their village Batoche. They settled in a lengthy fashion on both sides of the river.

Batoche was soon to be recognized and accepted as the Metis capitol. During the 1885 rebellion it would become the final, crucial battleground after earlier Metis victories against Canadian troops.

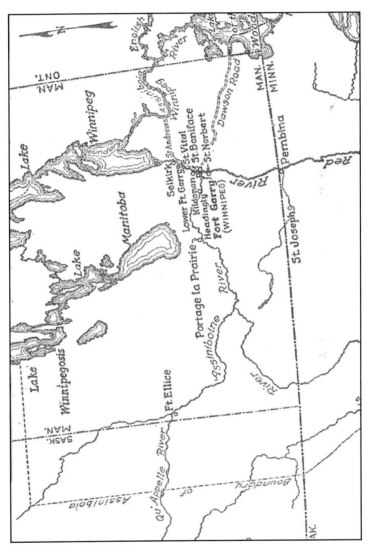

Pembina and Fort Garry area.

Chapter 2
UNREST AT FORT GARRY

Fort Garry was built by the Hudson's Bay Company between 1817 and 1822. It was situated at the confluence of the Red River and Assiniboine Rivers. The Metis people had reluctantly moved north from Pembina to the Fort Garry area when Pembina became part of the United States and the State of Minnesota as the U.S. And Canadian border was established at the 49th parallel.

Still considered and referred to as Rupert's Land, in this area the Metis proposed a bill of rights for Rupert's Land. It was considered a remarkable document. Though native peoples overwhelmed by whites in North America had often prepared demands as the basis of negotiations, they had little in common with the bill drafted by and in behalf of the Metis of the Northwest. It was notable in another respect as it offered a feasible program for union with the Dominion, and at the same time to protect the interests of all. No Englishman, Canadian, Frenchman, American or Indian could complain that his traditions or economic needs were ignored. The concept that, if Rupert's Land would become part of the Canadian Dominion, it would do so only as a full-fledged, self-governing Province was born at this time.

Louis Riel designed the flag himself to represent his Metis people and the Provincial Government. The flag carried the golden symbol of Medieval France on a pure white background which had originated with Samuel Champlain, French adventurer and explorer.

The Metis had good reason to believe that the ever-intrusive eastern government meant to interfere with their way of life, even possibly to subjugate them. In the Fort Garry area the virulent seeds of the upcoming rebellion would ultimately bear a very disruptive fruit. A major disturbing factor for the Metis in the Fort

Garry area was that they no longer had the benefit of the old river-lot principle. The government would answer complaints that the principle was now too awkward to administer and was therefore usually discouraged. But neither the land claims nor the river-lot principle seemed at all to be just a minor issue to the Metis peoples. Both were central to their way of life.

In November of 1869 during confrontations with English Canadians, Riel's men captured 13 of them, jailing them at Fort Garry. Riel and 120 of his followers ultimately seized Fort Garry. They held it till forcing the Dominion of Canada to negotiate terms. The result was the Province of Manitoba, officially created in 1870, with special rights for the Metis French. Riel can then be regarded as the father of Manitoba. There were also English-speaking mixed bloods in Fort Garry at the time who resented the French Metis.

During November Riel issued a proclamation inviting the English-speaking residents of the area to elect 12 representatives with his French council of Metis. 24 delegates to the first convention of the people of Rupert's Land assembled at Fort Garry with an armed guard of 150 Metis. The English were somewhat mollified as the British ensign was still flown over Fort Garry. The Metis decision that, if ever became part of the Dominion of Canada, it would do so, only as a full-fledged, self-governing province was born at this time.

One of the 13 men Riel had captured and jailed at Fort Garry was an Irish Canadian from Ontario Province named Thomas Scott. He would prove to be a source of hatred of the eastern Canadians for Riel. Scott later boasted that he himself would shoot Riel. There was a time that Scott and Riel met on a street at Fort Garry and Scott attacked Riel with his fists. Riel, no fighter, was rescued by onlookers. Scott continued as a trouble-maker and rabble rouser. He was finally arrested and jailed, continuing to threaten to kill Riel. The Metis council ordered a court-martial against Scott and had him brought before them. This immediately enraged the Province of Ontario.

Ultimately Scott was condemned to death for his threat of

murder. The culprit was condemned by a 4 to 3 verdict. The English-speaking community alerted to the verdict spent the night of March 3 and the next morning trying to save him. Although a Donald Smith and Father Lestance anxiously interceded, Riel was immovable. At noon, his eyes bandaged, with the Rev. Mr. Young beside him Scott was led into the courtyard and ordered to kneel in the snow. A firing squad of 6 Metis lined up before him. Three of the rifles held no bullets so the squad never knew who actually fired live rounds. Guilmette, a member of the firing squad came forward to administer the coup-de-grace, a bullet to the head. The Metis people like Indians, could be savage in a fight; in the ten months that they controlled Rupert's Land, Scott was the only person that they killed.

Thomas Scott and Louis Riel ceased to exist as men. They became symbols; Scott the Protestant, Riel the Catholic. The angry Ontario Province offered a $5,000 reward for the capture and prosecution of Scott's murderers, as they put it. One of Louis Riel's most fateful decisions at the time of Fort Garry's political unrest was to condone the execution. However justified that it may have been, that act inflamed anti-Catholic and anti-French feelings also leading to Riel's voluntary exile sometime later to the United States.

With the struggle in Rupert's Land for Dominion status, a Donald Smith emerged to sway the outcome. Louis Riel and other Metis leaders disagreed. Riel wished to incorporate a demand that Rupert's Land be admitted to the Canadian Dominion as a full-fledged, self-governing province.

The peoples of Rupert's Land were summoned by Riel to a large, snow-covered field near Fort Garry. There was no hall large enough to hold the huge turnout expected to hear Smith make his case for Canada and to decide and vote on what they wanted to do; a monumental decision. Swift Metis runners had carried Riel's proclamation calling the meeting far and wide to the most remote corners of the scattered settlements. There was, at this time, in the Red River settlements and outlying areas north of the boundary about twelve thousand people. Half were Metis and about four thousand were English half-breeds. There were only fifteen hundred whites and six hundred Indians.

As the huge crowd stamped their feet trying to keep warm in the icy temperature, Smith came forward on the platform and obtained the chairman's permission to make a personal statement – his first in the two days of the talks. His voice was friendly, his words carefully selected and simple. The speech was short. "I sincerely hope," he concluded, "that my humble efforts may in some measure contribute to bring about, peaceably, union and accord among all classes.

After lengthy and argumentative talks among the gathered people, thanks to Donald Smith's rhetoric the residents finally agreed that the Northwest Territory to be a part of the Dominion of Canada. Riel's demand regarding provincial status was unsuccessful.

Riel's followers admired him but he was unfamiliar with power and its use. Taking Fort Garry by force created great tensions and uncertainty among the English-speaking community. Also the Metis were not the only mixed-blood group; there were English-speaking mixed-blood groups as well whom Riel wanted to carry along with him. But the Metis were the best-organized and most cohesive, and they had moved first. They were highly resented by the Canadians from Ontario who had come to regard the Red River area as their natural, if future possession. There were threats made, often more empty than real, but how could Riel know? As the turmoil at Red River was just beginning to settle, there appeared to be another threat, from some English-speaking Ontarians living out on Portage la Prairie. Riel's men caught them, armed, as they were passing by Fort Garry, put them in prison in the fort; and this act ultimately led to the execution of Thomas Scott.

This was an ill-judged move. Whatever Scott may have been – a Protestant recently from North Ireland who made trouble wherever he went – one did not shoot people, not even by court-martial. Riel really never recovered from the disaster that the shooting of Thomas Scott brought in its train. The Manitoba delegates to Ottawa had to go through Toronto incognito, so inflamed had

Ontario opinions become against Riel and the Metis.

Even though he was regarded as father of Manitoba, in some ways he was, but he made mistakes and he had made a bad one. He knew his men and influenced and persuaded them; they admired him, but he was unfamiliar with power and its proper use. Taking Fort Garry had created great tension and uncertainty. The Metis were not the only mixed-blood sect; there were English-speaking bloods as well, whom Riel wanted to carry with him as well. But the Metis were best organized and moved first. They were resented by others, not the least Canadians from Ontario who had come to regard Red River and the Fort Garry areas as their natural, if future possessions. There were threats spoken, often more empty than real; but, how would Riel would have known about that? By late February, 1870, after negotiations with Canada had been started and a delegation to Ottawa had been arranged for the spring, and as the turmoil in Red River was just beginning to settle, there seemed to be another threat from English-speaking Ontarians living out in Portage la Prairie Riel's men caught them, armed, as they were passing by Fort Garry, though they were on their way home as it turned out, put them in prison in Fort Garry. This led to the seminal incident during the Fort Garry unrest – the unfortunate Thomas Scott trial and execution.

A military expedition was sent out west to show the flag and it forced Riel to go into hiding; though this was not the official intent. The men of the Ontario militia would never have allowed Riel to escape had they found him. Riel was in time convicted of the murder of Scott. The English in Ontario, now looking at Louis Riel as a monster, posted a $5,000 reward for his capture. He was eventually given amnesty by the Canadian Government on condition of five years banishment from Canada.

After the Scott incident and his banishment from Canada; Riel settled in Judith Basin in northern Montana. He applied for and soon became a school teacher in the summer of 1883. Father Damiani at St. Peter's Mission hired Riel to teach Indian boys at the Mission school. He took charge of the entire education program the next year when a girl's school was established.

THE NORTHWEST MOUNTED

In 1873, two years after reports of the Cypress Hills Indian massacre, where, after drunken sprees 16 whites involved in whiskey peddling, killed 40 Assiniboines including women and children, the Canadian Parliament created the most glamorous and effective law agency in their history. Originally the new force was called the 'Canadian Mounted Rifles', but to avoid being thought of as extremely militant, the designation of 'Northwest Mounted Police' was substituted.

The crest of the Northwest Mounted – a buffalo head – and its motto, *"Maintiens le Droit"* were selected. The original force, three divisions of 50 men each, was recruited largely in Ontario and mobilized at Fort Garry in October.

The 'Mounties' striking uniform consisted of a tight, scarlet red Norfolk tunic, black breeches and pillbox hata white helmet for dress occasions; high, black leather boots and overcoat and cape.

They were armed with a pistol with a white lanyard, a Snider carbine and a cartridge belt of ammunition. Years later their areas of peace-keeping expanded greatly; from the Border, prairies, the North-west Territories and up into the frigid Yukon Also, years later their designation was changed to 'The Canadian Mounted Police' and eventually in the 1900's their final and current designation, 'The Royal Canadian Mounted Police.'

The original 'Northwest Mounted' faced the Louis Riel-led Metis in the initial battle of the 1885 rebellion. It occurred at Duck Lake, Saskatchewan, some miles south of Prince Albert and the Metis capitol village of Batoche on March, 26, 1885. As a result of Riel's military commander, Gabriel Dumont's superior preparations and tactics, the Metis sharpshooters and snipers won the conflict, forcing Major Leif Crozier's Mounties into headlong retreat. (See chapter 6)

LOUIS RIEL AGE 39 .. Judy Loken

Chapter 3
LOUIS RIEL, HERO OR TRAITOR

Intelligent and deeply religious, Louis Riel was the fluent, intellectual spokesman, inspirational leader and catalyst for the 1885 Metis Rebellion in Canada's Northwest Territories – the only armed rebellion in Canada's history.

Louis Riel was destined to loom huge in the Canadian political, social and historical spectrum during the late 1790's and 1800's, culminating in 'armed rebellion' and ensuing bloodshed.

A controversial person, intelligent, fluent in two languages, French and English, Riel by nature was peace-loving and gentle, yet at times could burst into passionate rages. In fact, he had spent almost two years in a Quebec area asylum. Riel came to believe that his was a holy mission to lead his Metis people, and considered himself as the "prophet of the new world." He became more and more outspoken and convinced that God had chosen him to create a Metis 'homeland', completely independent of any federal control or interference with their lifestyle in the western prairies or forests.

Today, 128 years later, the Northwest Rebellion still engenders distinctly opposite views and opinions. Was Riel a hero- or a traitor? To the Canadian Government in Ottawa at the time he was thought of and represented as a "Benedict Arnold"; a traitor to his country by promoting and leading the movement for an independent Metis Nation.

Conversely, many Canadians, especially the Metis peoples, of whom there were thousands in the Saskatchewan area considered him a patriot a la "Nathan Hale" - "Give me liberty or give me death!"

After many decades, and generations, the Metis had been an

independent, self-sustaining people. They were a hardy river, prairie and wilderness sect, hunting, trapping and fur-trading as their time-honored way of existing in their special environment. Riel believed that their insurrection wasn't a rebellion but simply a resistance against an aloof and unsympathetic Government ignoring their complaints concerning the increasing incursions by white English settlers, taking up more and more of their land.

Employing Riel's leadership, fluency and intellectual skills, other Metis leaders prompted Riel to petition Ottawa for independence, but they were simply ignored. Thus the virulent seeds of insurrection were sown beginning in the 1870's.

Born in the Red River Metis settlement of Pembina in 1844, Louis Riel became educated in Berthier, Quebec where he began to study for priesthood in the Catholic Faith. He felt at first that the call to the priesthood would withstand the call to the prairies and forests of his Metis people. Well-educated, bilingual and Intelligent, Riel was thought of as a natural leader, even in his early twenties. Riel's father, Louis Riel the elder, known as the "miller of the Seinne" having built a flour mill on a tiny tributary of the Red River. Riel's mother was a Metisse, or half French, half Montagnais. The Montagnais were a northern tribe of moose hunters. They had once overcome the mighty Iroquois in a triumphant conflict. For his wife, Riel chose Julie Lajimodiere. Julie was the daughter of the famed "first white woman in the Northwest Territory and sister of the "first white child."

Young Louis had last seen his father after a trip to the prairies in 1858 at Pembina. Louis was fourteen at the time and leaving soon for Montreal and his priesthood studies. Archbishop Tache' of St. Boniface had been struck by the young Riel's intellectual precocity and religious ardor during his elementary schooling there and had suggested college.

Entering the Seminary, Riel's somber mien caused comments. He was admired as an unusually intent, serious scholar. After his father's death and bereavement, he shunned the company of others. Being one-eighth Indian, he was not identifiable as a Metis by anyone who did know his antecedents. At the time Louis was solidly built, strong and youthfully handsome. His features, somewhat sallow but not darkly pigmented, had not yet taken on the morose dignity that would distinguish it later. The intensity of his gaze was noticed and remarked upon by observers. He had deep-set brown eyes that would always be his most forceful physical feature. He was an inch or so under six feet, although that feature would be debated by many. His hair was brown and became darker as he passed into manhood; swept back in luxuriant waves from his broad forehead. Later he was to affect the "burnsides" look, his face thinned out somewhat and later grew a mustache and full beard.

Strangely his eyes were usually still, as he was character-ristically nervous. When among company he was unable to sit quietly, but had to rise and walk restlessly about the room. He would gesture, interrupt other's talk- or suddenly become silent amidst a tirade of his own then at times even quitting the room without explanation, ignoring his companions.

Louis spent ten years in Montreal until his widowed mother sent for him indicating that she needed him. He returned to the Northwest without continuing or completing his religious education. He was eager to return to the prairies despite his strong call for a religious career. His poet-mystic mind was impatient of dogma and canon law.

On the way home in 1868, he stopped off for a month or so at St. Paul, Minnesota working as a sales clerk in a general store to earn some money to take to his mother. His evenings were taken up with excited talk with some of the Red River Metis who brought news of the mounting unrest north of the US Border.

Most Metis men matured early, but Louis had little experience on the hunt where men were made, and had known few hardships. He was a mediocre horseman. He was clumsy with hands un-dexterous. He couldn't shoot straight and used liquor sparingly. He was nearly 40 when he married. To his colleagues at the Metis Council he was considered the brain – and their voice. Fluent in public, he could argue, debate in three languages – French, English and Cree. Later, when the fate of British North America hung upon the whim of Riel, he refused to foreswear allegiance to the Queen.

Riel began to dream of a new, French-Catholic state in the west. The Saskatchewan country, where Catholic Metis and Indians were in the majority, was a possibility he mused. or perhaps even Dakota or Montana Territories.

He sought to be half medicine man, half Christian mystic, turning to God. In 1876 he was decoyed by friends into St. Jean de Dieu Asylum and kept there by force until he could be committed, under the name of Louis David Riel. He later moved to Beauport Asylum near Quebec. There he remained until 1878. Riel showed signs of paranoid schizophrenia, grandiose illusions, bound together to form sometimes plausible, sometimes incredible delusional patterns. He was later released after almost two years in asylums.

A controversial individual, intelligent as well as masterful, Riel was gentle and peace-loving by nature, yet capable of passionate rages. He came to believe that he had a holy mission to lead the Metis people, considering himself the "Prophet of the New World." He felt that God had chosen him to create an independent Metis homeland on the Canadian western prairies and to inspire them to protest against the incursions by growing numbers of white English settlers into the historic Metis homeland and hunting grounds.

Riel was also showing at this time, probably unconsciously, some sense of history. In effect he was attempting to recreate, on a minute scale in the Western wilderness, the Jesuit-dominated 17th Century state of New France. His new Saskatchewan, like New France, was to be a consecrated state its chief characteristics piety and dedication to militant propagation of the faith.

After spending some years in Montana under his banishment from the Dominion for the Fort Garry rebellion and the controversial Thomas Scott trial and execution, he concentrated his time and efforts to supervise the Mission's children's schools. Louis looked about him at the land of the Metis; then turned back to Marguerite. It soon would be time for Mass.

The English-speaking half-breeds as well as French Metis

combined to persuade Riel to return to Canada in the summer of 1884. The felt that Riel's leadership ability, intelligence, education and fluent command of both French and English would aid his Metis people in the increasingly troublesome non-understanding emanating from Ottawa. By bringing Riel back to Canada.

In the summer of 1884 during one Sunday at Mass Riel was called from the Church. There was someone to see him and it was important. This was unprecedented and Louis was annoyed. He walked to the Mission yard to find all the youngsters excited and surrounding four mounted men.

The visitors dismounted, hurried to Louis and presented themselves: Gabriel Dumont, "Prince of the prairies," and the most prominent and respected Metis at Batoche, was already known to him. Two others were Metis from St. Laurent, Moiese Ouellette and Michel Dumas; and the fourth, an English half-breed from Prince Albert, James Isbister. They had ridden 680 miles from the Saskatchewan settlements to ask Riel to come back with them and take charge of their campaign for redress of their grievances against Canada. Louis's heart leaped. He directed the visitors to his cabin and hurried back to the little Church. He knelt and gave thanks; his mission was confirmed.

He welcomed the four men as guests but asked for a day to give his answer. His written answer given to Dumont the following morning was straightforward and practical. The invitation honored Louis, he wrote, because both French and British half-breeds had extended it. He accepted it. Seeing his poor conditions they now knew how much he had struggled for the whole Northwest peoples how and how little he worked for himself. They returned with twice the confidence in him as when they left their followers at Batoche.

Upon returning to Saskatchewan with Dumont and the others they arrived at the metis capitol of Batoche. Riel, Dumont and their companions upon returning to Batoche were greeted enthusiastically with gunfire, cheering and singing by about seventy or eighty people, smiling, happy as their hopes of improved conditions were raised.

Chapter 4
A PLACE CALLED BATOCHE

The Metis refugees established prosperous farms in the west, naming their settlement after a Metis trader, Xavier Letendre, whose nickname was "Batoche." Like their aboriginal brothers, the Metis subsisted largely by hunting buffalo. But the bison were disappearing in the early 1880's from the western prairies. The Metis began seeking education and other means to adapt to the changing economy. Also they began to encounter problems similar to the ones they had experienced along the Red River, as white settlers threatened to take over their land. Metis appeals for help from the Federal Government in Ottawa again were met with silence or evasion from the Dominion authorities. This standoffishness and ignoring of their needs was to produce a volatile environment.

The Metis people almost unanimously regarded Riel as a self-sacrificing patriot and were ecstatic when he agreed to return to Batoche and lead them in petitioning Ottawa for their grievances. To white settlers in the area, they almost to a man considered Riel a bloodthirsty rebel and mad messiah. To the Metis Riel became their spiritual and political head. He pledged to rule and represent all area residents with compassion and justice for all without prejudice. Ten miles from Batoche, as the Riel party crossed the plain approaching the broad valley of the South Saskatchewan River, 70 Metis streamed out to meet them, cheering and firing salutes. They escorted Riel to the settlements where hundreds more awaited his arrival.

Returning to Western Canada, Riel found the Metis village of Batoche to be suitable as their new Capitol. Batoche was about 40 miles southwest of the fast-growing English community of Prince

Albert along the South Saskatchewan River. The Metis lived in log cabins, clean and comfortable, straggling along the riverbank for a mile or two. A trail led from the prairie down to the river and ferry, named "Batoche's Crossing." Stores, farms and homes were clustered along both sides of the river. Their new Capitol, called Batoche would be where the Metis would make their last, valorous stand against insurmountable military odds.

Batoche had been built at a bend on both sides of the South Saskatchewan River where it was about 100 yards wide. It was a cabin-occupied village of about 500, with a few homes and stores along both sides of the river for about three miles. A distance away, on high-ground on the east side of the river was the cemetery and St. Antoine-de-Padoue Catholic Church. In that simple village Riel still believed that God would protect the Metis. There he chose to make their brave stand.

Without agreeable and effective representation in Ottawa, their only resort had been letters, memos and petitions. The Department of the Interior was always slow to respond and even slower to act, leaving the Metis feeling much as they had a decade and a half earlier before at Red River. They were still a beleaguered, ignored and vulnerable people by the Canadian Government in Ottawa.

Other grievances remained, ones which the Canadian Government could or would do little about. The past life of the Metis as carriers and freighters with their prairie ox carts for the Hudson's Bay Company was mostly gone now with steamboats on the Saskatchewan River and the new Canadian Pacific Railway beginning to spread to the west. With the life-sustaining buffalo now gone, the Metis took ill to the farming lifestyle. This led to hunger and a growing restive people in the Saskatchewan Territory by 1884. In Feb. 1885 with no answer to petitions, Riel proposed that he return to the U.S. Angry protests filled the room and he consented to remain as their leader.

GABRIEL DUMONT: "PRINCE OF THE PRAIRIES"

The leading and most prominent Metis citizen outside of Louis riel at the time of the rebellion was Gabriel Dumont. At only 32 years of age his word was law. As trouble and unrest surfaced he was chosen as the Adjutant General of all the Metis forces involved when the rebellion began. Dumont, stocky and possessing a commanding aura, was a legendary buffalo hunter and the organizer and leader of the annual buffalo hunt until 1881.There were two annual buffalo hunts, in June and September or in October, weather permitting. Dumont was one of the best shots among the Metis. As a tactician and guerilla fighter he was a natural, crafty and highly intelligent military leader. Years after the rebellion and before his return to Canada in 1893 after his amnesty he joined the Buffalo Bill Wild West Show as a crack marksman.

Dumont had the innate ability to read the prairie like a book. At age 25, already a skilled bowman, ingenious on the trail, an expert horse breaker, but above all his generosity and unselfishness earned him the title of "The Prince of the prairies." He was multilingual, speaking several Indian tongues and French, but could not understand English nor speak it. Gabriel had the standings among the Metis to curb Riel if he chose to, but sincerely loved him and rarely disputed his decisions – never in public. It was an omnipresent grief and regret for Dumont's wife, Madeleine that she had never given him a son. Years later as Dumont raged furiously through the brush and hunted out fugitive caves in the coulees, fruitlessly seeking Riel, she accompanied him faithfully with the food, clothing and blankets they had gathered for other Metis children.

At the young age of 25 Dumont became chief of the semi-annual buffalo hunt, with about three hundred followers from two or three consolidated buffalo-hunt camps.

Dumont had acquired – no one knew how, because few even among the Indians could still do it -the age-old trick of "calling" buffalo, and at times had lured as many as a dozen into a trap. His ingenuity on the prairies and trails, his skills (he was the camp "doctor") and unlike most Metis a swimmer. But above all his unselfish generosity made him the "Prince of the prairies" to his people. Gabriel was a man of medium height, with heavy shoulders and head but the trim torso of a horseman and with an open and kindly, almost childishly innocent face.

When a member of his camp on a road job for which Gabriel had contracted for became a father, Gabriel gave him a horse and cart and filled the cart with meat. When this particular road job was finished, Gabriel bought from his own pay two sacks of food and gave them to the priest for distribution to the elderly and needy of the parish. On the hunt he habitually made a "free run" and donated eight or ten buffalo to the poorer families in his camp.

But as a chief he was a severe disciplinarian who brooked no violation of the prairie code and frowned even on mischief. The tongue-lashing he gave some youths for interfering with a herd became famous among his people, and he once administered a bad beating to an Indian and Metis who had "gone before" on the hunt. On another occasion, by fining and seizing the equipment of a Hudson's Bay Company hunter who had tried to get a head start on the Batoche brigade, he precipitated an incident which brought the Mounties hurrying to the scene and inspired scareheads about rebellion in the Canadian press.

The trouble began when Lawrence Clarke, the company factor at Fort Carlton, complained to the Governor of Manitoba, that Gabriel and his Metis had enacted laws "of a most tyrannical nature" and were punishing violators of these laws with "criminal severity."

Leadership came naturally to Gabriel Dumont: his father and uncle had negotiated a peace pact with the Sioux, something no one was able to do before. And he was the sort of a man about whom legends grew. Before he was ten he had his first gun, a gift from his uncle as a reward for a display of courage. As a ten-year old Gabriel and his brother were busy building a smudge fire to discourage mosquitoes, when they heard a roar which Gabriel took to be the sound of an approaching band of Sioux. He ran to his father and demanded a gun which he could help to defend the camp. The noise was that of a buffalo herd but Gabriel got the gun.

The historian, W. L, Morton, who grew up in Manitoba described the Metis buffalo hunt thusly: The hunters, each mounted n his best horse, rode out approaching the herd up-wind. When in position they charged in line at a captain's signal. They carried their rifles across the neck of his mount, and had a handful of powder in a pocket, his mouths full of balls. Each picked his animal and rode alongside. The gun was fired across the horse's neck. The Red River Metis hunter could bring down his prey up to 50 or 100 yards, though the shot was fired from close range.

A palm full of powder was poured down the gun's barrel, a ball spat into the muzzle, and the whole shaken home by knocking the rifle's butt on the thigh or saddle. His horse meantime had galloped ahead to overtake a new beast. And so it went to the thunder of hooves, the snorting and roaring of the herd in the dust of the summer prairie, an exciting hell-bent-for-leather way of life that would soon disappear into the mists of time.

Chapter 5
TO ARMS!

On March 18, 1885, the French settlements were electrified by a rumor: Lawrence Clarke, of Hudson's Bay Company, told some people that some 500 more Northwest Mounted Police were enroute to Saskatchewan and that Riel and other leaders would soon be under arrest. The cry, "To arms!" echoed through the villages as Metis horsemen seized their guns, mounted, and rode to Batoche to protect their chief, Louis Riel. The Metis Council, at Riel's urging, claimed itself as a Provincial Government. The Metis promptly took stores of guns and ammunition from two local stores. Riel rebuked them for theft and urged the owners to keep an account and "charge it." In March, Riel and his followers seized the Parish Church at Batoche, solidified their Provincial Government and demanded Fort Carlton's surrender. Moreover, Riel lacked the skill and communicating ability for so delicate an operation as raising large support from the Indian nations.

That night, Metis horsemen rode out to the prairies and cut the telegraph wires in two places. The Northwest rebellion, the last stand of the new nation of Louis Riel, had begun.

The Northwest Mounted Police, forerunners to the Royal Canadian Mounted Police, who would be involved in the 1885 fighting, were established in 1873 by Sir John Macdonald. Their headquarters were built at Regina and are still operational today. Fort Carlton, about 20 miles west of Batoche, had about 75 Mounties under Superintendent Major Crozier. Riel and the Metis Council served notice on Crozier that he must abandon Fort Carlton, and that they would be given safe passage out of the Saskatchewan Territory. At Crozier's urgent request, Prince Albert community contributed about 70 civilian volunteers to bolster

Carlton's garrison.

Anticipating wishes of Parliament, the Mounted Police had been strengthened and Sir John Macdonald had written to Donald Smith of the Hudson's Bay Company asking for the use of Fort Carlton for Crozier's Mounties. His request had been readily granted.

Riel made an impressive speech to the English community at Prince Albert prior to the outbreak of hostilities. His program was moderate. He asked that the Metis be given free title to the land they presently occupied and that the three territorial districts of Saskatchewan, Assiniboia and Alberta be raised to Provincial status. Riel believed that "God had prepared me for some great things." During the fall Riel's movement had been strengthened by adherence of whites and Canadians. Big Bear, chief of the Cree, headed a band of about 500 Indians to possibly aid the Metis.

Riel believed that armed blackmail, which had worked so well in Manitoba in 1869-70, could be effective in Saskatchewan in 1885, but Sir John Macdonald was not having it, not a second time, especially not a second time from Louis Riel. And, the Canadian Pacific Railway, almost finished now, was one solid reason why. Back in 1869 Riel had been master of Manitoba, and there had been no way Macdonald could get at him save by laborious negotiations. But in 1885 Macdonald and the Canadian Government had troops unloading at Qu'Appelle Station within eleven days of the first shooting outbreak by the Metis.

Thomas McKay, a Scotch half-breed and Hudson's Bay agent, went to Batoche in a courageous but fruitless effort to persuade the Metis from embarking on an open rebellion. Riel refused to consider McKay's pleas and also denied his request to meet with Major Crozier. "In answer to our petitions the Government sends police," Louis cried. Gesturing to the armed Metis, "These are my police!"

Riel repeated his notice to Crozier that he must abandon Fort Carlton and his headquarters at Battleford. The ultimatum, dated March 21 concluded: "In case of non-acceptance, we intend to attack you when tomorrow, Lord's Day is over; and to commence without delay a war of extermination upon all those who have shown themselves hostile to our rights. ... Major, we respect you. Let the cause of humanity be a consolation to you for the reverses which the government misconduct has brought upon you."

Only a fraction of the population of Canada's Northwest Territories actually became involved in the final catastrophic phase of the Metis movement. This was partially due to the fact that Riel, and not the much more militant Gabriel Dumont, was the supreme leader. It was also partially due to the decimation of the Blackfeet by starvation and disease, also, the noted missionary, Father Lacombe who persuaded the powerful Canadian tribe to keep the peace and not join the rebellion.

The French villages along the South Saskatchewan River, in which the trouble centered, contained about two thousand people. A few hundred in the Battleford district to the west and a few Indian bands which included about a thousand men, women and children, also were drawn into the conflict. But the whites in Prince Albert did not stick to see it through.

While the Canadian militia sloshed wearily westward toward the upcoming conflict, the Metis Provisional Government met daily, opening each session with a prayer composed by Riel. But Dumont chafed at such pious pastimes. He felt he should be in the field. His scouts had intercepted telegrams reporting the Canadians movements. Now we should be using guerilla tactics he advised Riel

Dumont's scheme was thoroughly sound. He wanted to disrupt the Canadian troops transport and supplies by dynamiting the Canadian Pacific Railways tracks in multiple places to interrupt the Canadian troops supplies and reinforcements. He also advocated making sudden descents upon the inadequately protected prairie outposts where food for the men and hay for the horses being stored in preparation for the Canadian troops northern march. The Canadian forces were exhausted, Dumont knew; later he commented that if he had been permitted to carry out his plans, "I could have made them so edgy that at the end of three nights they would have been at each other's throats." And he would prove the effectiveness of this night terrorism before the campaign ended.

But Riel refused to assent to guerilla warfare when Dumont first proposed it. His arguments now indicated that he still hoped the Metis outburst would be regarded as a demonstration and a threat, and that all avenues to peace were not closed. The Metis had friends among the advancing Canadians, he insisted. But Gabriel Dumont scoffed at this; "I wouldn't consider as our friends those who would join the English to kill and plunder us." "If you knew them," Riel retorted, "you wouldn't try to treat them this way. Besides your guerilla tactics were too much like the Indians."

Dumont yielded, but this time he grumbled, "I was convinced ", he said, "that from a humane standpoint mine was the better plan. But I had confidence in his faith and his prayers and that God would listen to him." Dumont's suggestions never were submitted to the Metis Council. Instead, Riel insisted upon taking up the time of that body with religious matters.

Some of the Canadian militiamen, like soldiers everywhere and any time began to wonder what were they doing here. The Metis it appeared were not ignorant savages, but tough and intelligent fighters. Moreover, such of their home life as the Canadians had seen indicated that they had something to fight for. They thought that perhaps the Metis were not the idle troublemakers, incurable malcontents and bloodthirsty Papists they had been pictured by Sir John Macdonald and the Orangemen of the Ontario Province.

"The feeling that the half-breeds had been wronged, that the Government had been criminally negligent, and that the politicians should be held accountable for the "whole trouble" was growing among the troops a newspaper correspondent wrote home.

The Metis were not alone in their troubles. Many Indians in the region were starving and having trouble adjusting to life on the newly-established reserves; and again, the Federal Government had turned a deaf ear to the Indian's concerns and needs. Cree chief Big Bear, the last of the plains' Indian leaders to sign a treaty with the Government, and another Cree Chief, Poundmaker, along with a few Dakotas, decided to join forces with Riel. But, on the other hand, a far greater number of Indians, such as Blackfoot chief Crowfoot, preferred to avoid risking a ruinous war. The coalition of the Metis and some 400 Cree and other indigenous tribes in the Saskatchewan region set the stage for the upcoming clashes with the Federal forces.

Chapter 6
DUCK LAKE: BAPTISM OF FIRE

Sir John Macdonald acknowledged in response to nervous inquiries in the House of Commons that there was a little trouble on the frontier, confirming fragmentary reports in Ontario of an uprising, plundering of stores and jailing of citizens. It was a minor disturbance, he said, and there was no cause for concern. That was March 23. The Prime Minister even joked, "Those people are always complaining. If you wait for a half-breed or an Indian to be contented, you may wait till the millennium."

The night of March 25, Gabriel Dumont led a small force to Duck Lake, a Metis community about midway between Batoche and Fort Carlton and on the edge of a small Cree Indian reserve. The store there was one of the largest in the district at the time, and in addition to its own stock, contained a large shipment of Government supplies destined for Indian agencies and police posts. Dumont's men partially looted the store for needed ammunition and supplies. At two o'clock in the morning of March 26th the Metis captured two scouts sent out by the Mounties Major Crozier and imprisoned them in the store. Because his scouts had not returned, Crozier sent Thomas McKay with an escort to bring the police supplies from Duck Lake to Fort Carlton. This party was met by Dumont and his men but was turned back after an argument.

When the rebuff was reported at Fort Carlton, Crozier set out for Duck Lake with a force of 56 Mounties and 43 volunteers from Prince Albert, most of them mounted. They took Crozier's only cannon, a little seven-pounder, and sleighs to bring back the supplies. This advance was a grave error in judgment as Colonel Irvine was less than fifty miles away, riding from Prince Albert with the reinforcements. But the supplies at Duck Lake were important.

In addition to the trouble at Duck Lake, the Indians were rising. Panic-stricken Prince Albert had lodged all their women and children in the Presbyterian Church and manse, surrounding them with a cordwood stockade. Anglo-Saxon settlers, their isolated farms in flames, were fleeing for their lives over snow-choked trails or in small boats on rivers full of drifting ice.

An emergency force of volunteers, about two hundred, were being armed, mounted and rushed south to the Montana line, beyond which lived thirty-two thousand Indians and Metis, potential allies of Riel. The Dominion appealed to the commanders of 1,680 United States troops in Dakota and Montana to help guard the boundary. The war for the west, begun fifteen years earlier on the Red River, had now entered its final desperate stage.

Mountie Major Crozier set out for Duck Lake with 56 Mounties and 43 Prince Albert civilian volunteers. Two miles from the Duck Lake trading post, Crozier's advance scouts discovered some Metis on a low hill 200 yards away. The rebels were lying prone on blankets, shielded by brush or hummocks of sod. Some, like Gabriel Dumont were on horseback in a small coulee. Snow was falling and visibility was poor.

Crozier halted his force and had the twenty supply sleighs drawn into a line across the road. At the end of his line, at a murderous close range, there stood a log cabin. If Crozier noticed the cabin he did nothing about it. Isidore Dumont, Gabriel's brother came forward with an Indian from the Metis hill position for a parley. Major Crozier, with a half-breed interpreter met them on horseback.

Major Crozier extended his hand to the unarmed Indian, but the Indian made a grab for the interpreter's rifle. The interpreter fired and Isidore Dumont fell from his horse, dead. Crozier glanced over to the Metis lines; they were moving and spreading around his left flank. He shouted a command to fire. With the first answering fire from the Metis lines Crozier realized that he had ridden into a well-planned ambush and his force was outnumbered. He then discovered that the log cabin to his right flank contained sharp-shooters who could pick off his men at the end of his line at will.

Now about 150 Metis warriors swarmed to the battlefield – at their head rode Louis Riel, mounted, unarmed, but holding at arm's length a foot and a half long Crucifix. During entire time of the Metis rebellion Louis Riel never fired a single shot. The Mounties fired at Riel but he was out of range. "In the name of the Father, Son and Holy Ghost answer to that", he cried. The Metis cheered as he continued to exhort them. With each shout from him his Metis sent another volley into the doomed crimson-jacked company on the field below.

As movement began around Crozier's left flank, he realized their dangerous situation and began pulling in his men for a retreat. He now knew that he would be lucky to escape a massacre. Now with his force hopelessly outnumbered, Crozier shouted out an order for a headlong retreat. The dead and wounded that could be reached were loaded on the sleighs, and then the troops fled without even rearguard firing to restrain or slow the surging Metis fighters. In the rebel lines an argument between Riel and Dumont raged. Dumont wanted to follow the fleeing troops and annihilate the entire force, but Riel countermanded the order - "In the name of God let them go; there has been too much bloodshed already." Dumont bowed to his wishes and there was no pursuit.

During the headlong retreat of Crozier's forces, Gabriel Dumont, now once again mounted, rode recklessly to within sixty yards of the troops. A bullet plowed a deep gash through his scalp and he fell, almost senseless; his horse, also wounded, jumped over his prone body and fled. Dumont struggled to get to his feet but dropped again, and a nearby Metis, Joseph Delorme cried out that their general had been killed. "Courage" Gabriel yelled. "As long as I haven't lost my head I'm not dead!" Another brother, Edouard Dumont, ran forward to drag him out of the line of fire but Gabriel sent him back to take command of their forces.

By order of their own officer, and without Crozier's approval, the civilian volunteers, maddened by the sniping from the cabin, made a foolhardy charge on it in which they lost heavily. Crozier was now hopelessly outnumbered and with his only cannon out of commission, he ordered a headlong retreat from the disastrous field of Duck Lake.

After being denied pursuit of the fleeing Government force, the wounded Gabriel Dumont was tied on his horse and the victorious war party rode back to the village, the men shouting with joy. Louis Riel, still waving his crucifix, was singing praises to God and the saints. They took with them a wounded civilian volunteer who had been left on the field by his mates; he was put under the care of the Canadian prisoners and when he had sufficiently recovered from his leg wound was released.

Back at Duck Lake, Riel summoned the people and lined up the victorious fighters for review. He offered a prayer of thanksgiving and ordered a special prayer and three rousing cheers for Gabriel Dumont, weaving wearily on his horse. "Give thanks to God" he commanded, "who gave us so valiant and brave a leader."

He then ordered the bodies of the rebel dead laid out in a nearby house and for the rest of the day led the people in prayer for their souls.

The victorious Duck Lake battle had lasted a half an hour. It cost the Canadian force 12 dead and 11 wounded out of ninety-nine engaged. Nine of the dead and four of the wounded were from the volunteer force, most being the victims of the rash attack on the cabin.

Five rebels, four Metis and one Indian had been killed and three, including Gabriel Dumont slightly wounded; their effective force had numbered about 200 fighters.

Among the rebels on the battlefield that victorious day, was a boy of fourteen, a distant relative of Gabriel Dumont whom the latter, without children of his own, often treated like a son. More than fifty years after the Duck Lake conflict his memory of it was still vivid. "You be scared like I was scared that day", he said. "You never forget either."

The boy, whose name was Alex, lay shivering for hours in the snow on top of the hill while the Metis awaited the Mounties and volunteers from Prince Albert. He remembered hearing his uncle

Gabriel cussing because his force was inadequate; Riel was not yet there with reinforcements, and Metis scouts had warned that Mountie Major Crozier was bringing about a hundred men.

"Nobody move" Gabriel had ordered, going among his men, forcing them to lie still and flat and far apart behind the clumps of brush. Then the police came – slow-moving, erect little shadows in the gray light amid the snow--seeming to ride toward them in the sky because in this sunless void there was no horizon.

The young, 14-year old lad, Alex, had no gun. He had joined Dumont's force uninvited; and now his assignment was to run down the hill and snatch cartridge belts from police casualties when and if Crozier's men were repulsed. Even if the enemy did not fall back, Alex boasted, that job would have been easy: "Any boy who couldn't outrun a bullet was no good." Foot racing was the chief recreation of the Metis boys.

Alex watched the abortive parley in the field; then ducked as the first Mountie's volley thudded into the hillside – far too low. He felt that he was a better marksman than the redcoats and volunteers, and it was too bad that he didn't have a gun. He had asked Gabriel, who had slain Blackfoot Indians, what it was like to kill a man. Gabriel told him that it was not much different from killing game. He remembered also, that when overconfident Metis had remarked that the police were only fair shots and the volunteers no good at all. Gabriel remarked grimly to Alex that men could very quickly learn to shoot well.

Early during the battle Gabriel lay prone beside Alex, crawled to the crest of the hill, and fired a dozen shots from his beloved Winchester carbine, aiming at the Mountie's gun crew. He disliked cannon, as his Metis had no defense against cannon shot. He inched himself back, reloaded, and mounted his horse to hurry to the left flank after the cannon was silenced.

Meanwhile, Riel had rode up and Alex watched, fascinated, as their chaplain-in-chief rode back and forth waving his foot and a half crucifix, rallying his people.

Alex didn't see Gabriel shot from his horse, but he saw him staunching the flow of blood from his forehead with handfuls of snow. Dumont had crawled to his cousin, Auguste Laframboise, who was dying and weakly attempted to make the sign of the cross over his cousin.

Alex then woke up to his duty and joined the triumphant warriors who were stripping the dead volunteers of guns and cartridge belts and carrying the bodies into a cabin where they would be safe from marauding animals. Riel had sent word back to Prince Albert that no harm would befall anyone coming to recover the dead bodies. A couple of days when some men from Prince Albert arrived, the Metis helped them place the bodies in their wagons. The rebels got a dozen good rifles, some ammunition, eight horses, and five sleighs or wagons. But this recovery notwithstanding, Gabriel scolded because they had not captured Crozier's wretched little seven-pound cannon.

That night, although Colonel Irvine and the reinforcements had arrived, the police decided that Fort Carlton; and the volunteers, now aware of the Metis combat abilities, clamored to return to Prince Albert to defend their homes and families. Crozier decided to burn the fort an under the cover of the billowing smoke retire his force.

About two thousand Indians lived on reserves around Battleford, a hundred miles west of Batoche. The first to respond to Riel's appeal for joining his Metis forces were the Cree of Poundmaker's band. Poundmaker was one of the foremost chiefs of the tribe; intelligent, an orator, and handsome. He was more than six feet tall, slender, with a thin, sensitive face and an air of dignity.

Chief Poundmaker was respected by the whites, but his tribe had been troublesome at times and was now ripe for a rebellion. They resented the restraints of reservation life and the Government decree that rations, which had been insufficient anyway, were to be issued only to those who would do farm work. Poundmaker, in frustration was known to have said, "Of old, the Indian trusted in his God, and his faith was not in vain. He was fed, clothed and free from sickness. The white man came and persuaded the Indian that his God was not able to continue his care. The Indian took the white man's word and accepted this new God. Hunger, disease and death followed soon. Now the Indian will return to the God we know; the buffalo will come back and the Indian tribes will again live the life that God intended him to live."

Poundmaker's hungry Crees learned of the Duck Lake battle and victory from Metis messengers two or three days after it occurred. They then decided to move on Battleford to loot its stores. On March 30 they arrived at the town. On that same day and the next the first Indian outrage of the Northwest Rebellion was committed by a nearby band of Assiniboines. The rebel Assiniboines murdered their farm instructor and a bachelor farmer, and then took the trail to join with the Crees.

The people of Battleford and settlers in the vicinity had warning of the marauding Indians approach and fled to the fort. The town was some miles away, beyond the range of the fort's cannon, and could not be defended. The night of the Indian's arrival they began sacking the village, continuing for days until every house and store, including the large Hudson's Bay's post had been emptied, fired and destroyed. At Frog Lake, to the west of Battleford, Big Bear's war chief named Wandering Spirit, instigated a massacre of nine white settlers.

Chapter 7
FISH CREEK & CUT KNIFE HILL

Gabriel Dumont, ever the superior tactician and military leader, realized after the retreat, burning, and evacuation of Canadian forces at Fort Carlton, that they would be even more vulnerable. Eagerly approaching Riel he told him that there was a place he knew on the trail of the fleeing Carlton garrison where Crozier's forces would have to pass through a narrow gap in a thick grove of trees. Perfect for an ambush he suggested. "No", said Riel, once again, still hesitant to allow more bloodshed. A few years later in an account of the incident Dumont said, "We could have killed a lot of them but Riel, who was always restraining us, opposed the ambush and further loss of life."

Duck Lake battle was considered the initial battle of the Northwest Rebellion. Among historians the general agreement is that the battle was strategically a defeat for the Canadian forces. In the aftermath, losing to Riel's Metis force came as a great shock to Colonel Irvine, Crozier's immediate superior, who felt that Crozier's officerial prowess and judgment had been overruled by his impulsiveness not waiting for Irvine's reinforcements to arrive.

Early on the morning of April 24, General Frederick Middleton led a force of Canadian militia northwest toward Batoche. As Middleton's column broke camp his English half-breed scouts found the sign of Metis horsemen and raced back to report their findings.

When the battle of Fish Creek officially opened the element of surprise for which Dumont had worked so carefully for, rested with the Canadians.

Dumont had warned and instructed his Metis horsemen to stay off the road and disperse to ride through the grass so as to leave no trail or sign for Middleton's force. But, he could not watch them all, and some of the irresponsible young warriors could not resist the fun of a chase on horseback after a few stray cattle, up and down the main road.

Gabriel and his little company of mounted men, enroute to their hiding places in the coulees, were unaware that they had been betrayed by carelessness, rode straight into a deadly silent Canadian advance guard with rifles at ready, and had to run for their lives. One or two of the Metis horsemen were felled with the first Canadian volley and others fled the field of battle in a sudden panic. Gabriel rallied the fifteen riders who remained, had them dismount, and made a stand in a thicket which held the Canadians off long enough to prevent complete disorganization of his command.

As it was, when he finally got back to the ravine in which his main force had been stationed, he found only forty-seven of the one hundred and thirty men he had left there. This gave Dumont only sixty-two on the battlefield, with a few more engaged in isolated sniping on the flanks of the Canadian column. At this stage in the conflict he was outnumbered six to one; when the fight ended nearly twelve hours later the odds against his forces was ten to 0ne. Dumont and Middleton's force opened fire on each other. The scouts dismounted and began firing into the coulee, and the main body of Canadians advanced to the coulee's edge. The Metis, hidden in the coulee pounded Gen. Middleton's men with one devastating fusillade before withdrawing into cover and restricting themselves to sniping in order to conserve their dwindling ammunition supplies.

A Metis horseman started on a dead run for Batoche to bring back the men who had been permitted to return with Louis Riel, and to attempt to round up deserters and persuade them to get back in the fight. Dumont was determined to make a stand, though the loss of the element of surprise upon which he had counted so heavily on had almost brought disaster. His forces still had the advantage of position however; and he had made a shrewd guess as to the mettle of the green troops and of the temper of their overcautious commander, General Middleton.

With half of his force on the opposite side of the river, Middleton was unable to bring his full numerical superiority to bear on the Metis positions. One of his artillery batteries opened fire on the Metis with little effect, although well-fired cannonades did succeed in driving away Dumont's Cree Indian allies before their full weight could be added to the battle.

Meanwhile, four miles upstream and across the river, Middleton's left column heard the cannonades fire and hurried north, soon to encounter a messenger from Middleton ordering it to cross and come to his aid. But this was a clumsy operation with only a scow and rafts in a swift-running river full of ice, and it took several hours to get part of the column to the east bank.

Strung out along the coulee's edge, silhouetted against the sky, the militia fired a vast amount of ammunition at their enemies, succeeding mostly in showering tree branches across the ravine. But when they pushed their guns to the coulee's edge to try to fire down at the concealed enemy, they suffered heavy casualties. The only targets the militia could clearly see were the Metis' tethered horses. They slaughtered about 50 of them.

Dumont's preparations in the ravine soon paid off in mounting Canadian casualties. Bypassing the thicket from which his fifteen stalwarts had directed a slow but appallingly accurate fire, and attempting to surround it, the leading elements of the Canadian force promenaded in orderly ranks over the crest of the coulee – then broke and fell back in dismay as they were met by a decimating volley from riflemen they couldn't see. Two cannon were rushed forward but it was soon found that they could not be placed on the lip of the ravine because their crews were outlined against the sky. The guns could not be aimed accurately and the shrapnel shells fell harmlessly far beyond the rifle pits, most of which were less than a hundred yards below the hilltop.

Middleton's distrust of his raw recruits appeared to be justified in the early phases of the battle. When a popular officer fell while urging his men into a charge, there was a moment of panic; but the young militiamen soon settled down and began to fight for their lives. The aging General rode into the front line and a bullet tore through his fur cap. He saw the shot fired and swore that the marksman was Gabriel Dumont. That might have been true, Gabriel acknowledged in a subsequent account of the fight, "but he can congratulate himself I didn't recognize him." Gabriel didn't know how many Canadians his Winchester accounted for because he took cover after each shot but, he said," I couldn't have missed often."

After some hours passed, the sixty-two Metis and Indians dwindled to fifty-four through casualties, desertions or the dispatch of messengers; but they still held more than four hundred white troops back of the hilltop. Middleton had no clear idea of the enemy's strength. He estimated it all the way from one hundred and twenty-five to three hundred.

It began to rain. The Metis were fairly comfortable in their brushy shelters in the game trails and draws, besides they were used to discomfort; but the Canadians were miserable. One group, after a daring charge on the rebel line failed, was pinned down for three hours in six inches of water in a marshy hollow as the rain poured down.

It was the Canadians first battle of the campaign and for most of them the first combat anywhere. Some gagged as they saw the rain drip red from torn bodies. They stared horror-struck at jagged ugly wounds in bellies and heads; not all the Metis had rifles and some were using muzzle-loading shot-guns into which they poured irregularly shaped scraps of lead or broken horseshoe nails.

The American rebels at Breeds Hill had used similar missiles in their rusty duck guns and the British had complained that it was shockingly bad form. But 110 years after the so-called "Battle of Bunker Hill" British commanders were still forwarding their soldiers in a solid, meaty phalanx into the close-range, murderous fire of eagle-eyed and un-gentlemanly colonists.

About noon the Canadians tried a general advance but they failed once again. After that the fight settled down into dreary hours of sniping, which was the Metis' forte. Some of the metis stragglers returned, entering the ravine far above the battle scene and worming their way back to the rifle pits and trenches. Their morale was high. Isidore Dumas began to sing "Malbrouck", the derisive dirge which 18th-century France had chanted for Winston Churchill's ancestor, the Duke of Marlborough and everyone joined in on a roaring chorus. The sun came out briefly and some of the Metis called attention of their fellows to the first yellow and purple blooms of the spring wildflowers.

Gabriel Dumont then began to joke. "Don't be afraid of bullets," he said, "They won't hurt you." Then he nonchalantly picked off a foolish young Canadian officer who had come to the crest of the hill to observe the situation. The Metis laughed as they heard the dying officer sobbing like a child.

The Canadians threw hundreds of rounds of ammunition and scores of cannon shells into the coulee without aiming; the Metis never wasted a single round. Nevertheless the Whites mass-charging half-hearted as they were, worried Dumont because they caused a drain on the rebel's limited supply of ammunition. In mid afternoon he learned that Middleton's reinforcements had begun to arrive, and at that time he had only seven cartridges left for his Winchester.

Eighty more Metis were riding hard from Batoche, but if the Canadians chose to attack now the rebels probably couldn't hold them back .Gabriel tested the wind and decided on a daring gamble. As a new line formed on the enemy's right flank, he ordered the prairie grass and brush fired, and told the Metis to charge under the cover of the billowing smoke. The heavy atmosphere of the day's rain held the smoke close to the ground as they swarmed, screaming savagely out of their gun pits. Crouching like Indian raiders, they raced to within a few yards of the Canadians, dropping prone and fired point-blank into the faces of the milling whites, then raced back to their ravine. The Canadians, choking in the smoke, gathered up their casualties and re-formed their lines; they did not break and run as Dumont had hoped they would – but on the other hand they did not launch the all-out attack they had formed. Once again as it would be displayed constantly, Gabriel Dumont's brilliant grasp of a military situation and tactics would prove superior.

The eighty-man reinforcements arrived from the Batoche village, led by Gabriel's brother Edouard. Their comrades, who had been lying cramped in the same position for ten hours, cheered wildly.

It began to rain again and to grow dark. The Canadians chafed with impatience and some of their officers begged Middleton to order an attack by the whole force. In retrospect, this would have quickly won the battle, but the cautious Middleton was unwilling to accept the responsibility for the losses it would entail. Instead, again he tried half-measures, splitting off a part of his force for a flanking movement up the ravine while the others maintained a cursory fire from the front. The Metis contemptuously ignored the harmless shooting from the hilltop, swung their sights on the approaching flanking column and quickly drove it back.

Desultory firing continued for another hour, by which time it was too dark for either side to see the enemy. The Canadians began to withdraw from the field of battle and the Metis rose to their feet and jeered. But they had had a narrow escape and they lost no time getting to what horses they had left; more than fifty of their horses had been killed.

One wildly jubilant party of about thirty Indian warriors rode almost into the Canadian's lines to yell and shriek insults. A British medical officer had abandoned his kit in the retreat; it contained two bottles of brandy in which the Metis solemnly drank to their benefactor's health, with the grinning Gabriel Dumont proposing the toast.

Neither "army" had eaten since dawn. Now, at a respectable distance from each other, they grabbed their rations and tried to draw aching limbs before the campfire. Gabriel debated the wisdom of a night attack, but with the weather being so bad and his Metis warriors being too tired; it was decided that all would return to Batoche.

The happy Metis had won the first encounter of the Canadian Army and the rebels. They had fought the troops to a standstill and their unexpected stiff resistance so thoroughly frightened Gen.

Middleton that he kept his force immobilized at this spot for two weeks; waiting for more men and ammunition to arrive. Arranging for the removal of his wounded was an important aspect of the war the Canadian command had forgotten, and a makeshift ambulance was created on the field.

The casualty figures told the story. The Metis rebels had lost only six men – four dead (two of them were Sioux Indians) and two wounded. But the Canadian casualties totaled fifty, more than ten percent of the number engaged on their side. Ten of these, including an officer, were killed and forty, four of them officers, were wounded, some grievously.

The day of the Fish Creek conflict the siege of Battleford was lifted by Colonel Otter's Second Division. The Indian's who had surrounded the fort fled before the troops arrived, and the ordeal ended for five hundred people penned for nearly a month in an enclosure less than 200 yards square.

The next day at Batoche Dumont learned that Riel had led the women of the village in prayer from dawn to dusk on the 24th. Dumont was grateful; undoubtedly, he told Louis that the prayers had brought victory to his Metis force. Gabriel was one of the most modest of men (except when it concerned his marksmanship with his Winchester) ever to administer a sound licking to a British general. Riel of course, congratulated Dumont for his brilliant leadership in taking a vastly outnumbered force and defeating Middleton's Canadians.

CUT KNIFE HILL

The extent of Chief Poundmaker's personal guilt in the sacking of Battleford was far from clear. Unquestionable there was danger that the Indians on his reserve, delighted with their success in looting every white establishment for fifty miles around that town, would soon join forces with Louis Riel's Metis forces at Batoche. Therefore British Colonel Otter decided that as soon as his 2nd Division had rested from its long hike he would teach Chief Poundmaker's Crees a lesson.

Like every decision made so far in the Canadian's campaign (and every one made in Ottawa before the troops were sent west), Otter's was thoroughly unwise. But for the forbearance of Chief Poundmaker it could have cost him his whole command; fortunately the soft-spoken dignified Cree Chief, like Riel, had no taste for slaughter.

Colonel Otter started from Battleford in the afternoon of May 1st with three hundred and twenty-five men, including a detachment of about seventy-five Northwest Mounted police. "Artillery" consisted of two seven-pound cannon and a Gatling gun, one of the three machine guns being tried out by the Northwest field force. The column marched until seven o'clock, camped for four hours, and went on again in moonlight. The plan was to surprise Poundmaker's camp at daybreak. Otter's scouts had reported that Poundmaker had three hundred and fifty braves; but actually only a couple hundred of them had firearms. The Indian camp had been anticipating Otter's attack. One of them told a white friend that he had been eating very lightly because the Indian braves had learned that filled intestines increased the chance of fatal abdominal wounds from bullet or arrow.

The Crees had been camped in the valley of cut knife creek, named for a famous victory over a Sarcee chief, thirty-eight miles south of Battleford. Just before Otter's troops arrived the Indians had move to a nearby plateau which was crowned by Cut Knife Hill, and a sentry on the hill was the first to see the advancing troops and warn the camp. The first alarm found only about fifty braves ready for action. They raced up the hill and took positions in the brush.

Col. Otter formed his men into a wedge. Two lines of soldiers and police faced the two ravines. The volunteers and militia guarded the rear, facing a marsh. Otter's men immediately cut loose with the Gatling gun and two seven-pound and did considerable damage to the swiftly-emptying tipis; but the Canadians made the fatal mistake of waiting on the hilltop until their full force was assembled instead of taking immediate advantage of their initial gains. Within moments the tipis were empty and the braves had taken up their positions – as swift, as deadly and as invisible as rattlesnakes. Twenty minutes after the first shots had been fired the Canadians became surrounded on three sides and their front rank was being methodically cut to pieces by hidden Indian sharpshooters. It was apparent that the Indians had planned it all and that the whites once more had stupidly and recklessly walked into a trap.

The Gatling gun, though it fired several thousand cartridges, was ineffective because its two-man crew couldn't see what they were shooting at. The two seven-pound were all that saved Otter from disaster, and after a hundred-odd shells had been fired both guns collapsed because their wooden carriages, rotten with age, collapsed into pieces. At one time, a shell from one of the guns narrowly missed annihilating a company of Canadians who had been sent forward into an exposed position.

The Indians were using an age-old trick, raising their war bonnets or scraps of clothing on sticks and picking off the Canadians when they rose from a prone position to fire. Hand-to-hand conflict developed for the first time in the rebellion when a group of Crees, yelling insanely, rushed the gun crews. This attack was beaten off with the firepower of the Gatling gun and the Indians were forced into a headlong retreat which could have become a rout if the Canadians dared to leave their position.

The Indians fought in small groups. One chief, "Fine Day" went to the top of Cut Knife Hill to direct a Cree counterattack. One group would run forward, attack the soldiers, and then rush back to the ravine before the soldiers could get them. As soon as the soldiers tried to attack the Indians on one side, another group of warriors would rush out of a second ravine and attack them from behind. Otter could not order a general attack because he had no idea where they were or their numbers.

The battle continued for more than seven hours. The Crees slowly closed the gap on the fourth side of the hill, and shortly after noon, with his force virtually surrounded, one cannon useless and the other nearly so, Colonel Otter acknowledged defeat and ordered an escape route to be cleared.

This was very difficult to accomplish and caused the heaviest losses of the day, but with the aid of the Gatling guns death-dealing firepower they managed to successfully fall back and ultimately decided to retire from the field of battle completely.

As the soldiers were crossing the marsh some of the warriors started to mount their horses to pursue them and attack. Chief Poundmaker however, asked them to let Otter's retreating men leave. As they respected Poundmaker they allowed them to leave and return to Battleford. Some historians believe that only this prevented an outright massacre of Colonel Otter's forces.

The battle of Cut Knife was the native's most successful fight during the Northwest Rebellion. They had the advantage of being in their own territory, but had some disadvantages. They were outnumbered, attacked by surprise, and short on ammunition. Fourteen of Otter's soldiers were wounded, and eight killed, including one abandoned and mutilated by Indian women. Three natives were wounded and five killed, including a Nez Perce who had come north from the U. S.

The battle also instilled in some of Otter's men a new respect for the enemy. Otter expected Poundmaker's people to be caught off-guard and demoralized and to quickly surrender. Despite suffering their greatest reverse during the campaign, the weight of numbers and better supplies favored the Northwest field force. In just a few weeks, the starving Cree went to Battleford to make peace with Major General Middleton. Fine Day, the Cree war chief who had directed the battle, escaped to the United States. Poundmaker was arrested and jailed. Lt. Colonel Otter survived the battle and remained at Battleford. Otter had one of the two new Gatling gun machine guns at Battleford. It hadn't helped him very much during the Cut Knife Hill conflict, but Gen. Middleton didn't know that. Thus ended the battle of Cut Knife Hill.

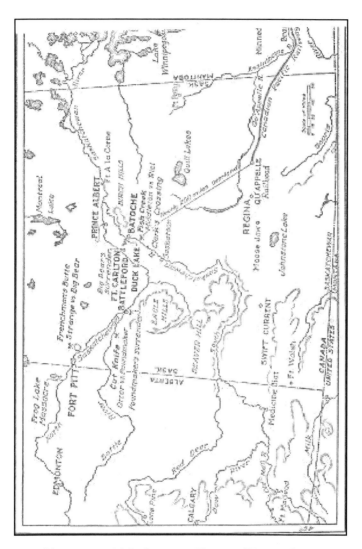

Conflict Area 1885. *Strange Empire/Howard.*

Chapter 8
LOUIS RIEL'S LAST STAND

Canada's Northwest rebellion reached its climax in May 1885, as the Government's army closed on the mixed-blood Metis provincial capital, the tiny village of Batoche. In the arena of world conflicts, the battle of Batoche was merely a small skirmish, yet it played an important part in Canadian history. It was the largest and longest battle to take place on the western prairies of Canada, and its political and social repercussions still affect many of that nation's institutions today. Of the Northwest rebellion's five major engagements, Batoche was by far its most significant. Some historians, in fact, have concluded that the Battle of Batoche is every bit as consequential as the 1876 George Custer's battle at the Little Bighorn.

In the face of the growing dissent and threat from Louis Riel and his Metis fighters, the Canadian Government was not idle. Minister of the militia and defense, Adolphe Caron, immediately ordered additional Canadian regulars prepare to entrain for the Northwest Territory.

Colonel Irvine, the Commissioner of the Northwest Mounted field force, was bottled up in Prince Albert, some 25 miles north of Batoche. He had available about one third of the five hundred Mounties who were nominally under his command in the Northwest Territories. Upon General Middleton entering the country, Irvine came under his command and jurisdiction. Twice Col. Irvine sent word to Gen. Middleton that he was awaiting his command to take to the field. Once, he even suggested when he heard of Middleton's planned march north, that a concerted attack be made upon Batoche by the militia from the south and the Mounties from the north.

For weeks Middleton didn't even report his whereabouts to Irvine, and when he received Irvine's wise suggestion for a joint attack he merely ordered him to remain where he was. When Irvine one day led a reconnaissance in force he was met by a messenger from the General to return to base.

As a traditional British officer, he was not accustomed to leading inexperienced militiamen. Middleton represented the elite of the British officer corps. He surrounded himself with British regular officers. He was physically courageous, even foolhardy, but he was also cautious and unwilling to risk very many casualties. That caution in the coming days would lead to some blunders.

In April Middleton moved out with 400 men from fort Qu'Appelle, adding militiamen to his force as he headed north. His troops numbered about 800 by the time he reached Clarke's Crossing on the South Saskatchewan River. There, he divided his field force into two columns, with one crossing to the west side of the river, the other remaining to the east. Both columns then began the march to Batoche where the Metis were entrenched and waiting.

Meanwhile Dumont's scouts had been keeping an eye on Middleton's force from the time it left Fort Qu'Appelle. Dumont insisted to Riel that he didn't want to stand and fight at Batoche. He was in favor of attacking the Canadian force after they had crossed the river and then pursuing guerilla warfare against Middleton's slow-moving columns. Riel initially disagreed but later relented allowing Dumont to put his plan into action. All of the 150 men he placed at Dumont's disposal knew the terrain well, where highly mobile, and able to strike quickly in surprise attacks. (Then followed the Fish Creek action described in Chapter seven.)

After the Fish Creek battle, Middleton's command was shaken. The Canadian advance was stalled for two weeks while the raw recruits in his army were trained for the coming attack on Riel's capitol village at Batoche. On May 7, his army now better prepared, he felt, resumed its march toward Batoche

To take the Metis village, Middleton devised a coordinated two-prong assault both from the river and by land. Prior to his arrival, he had ordered the Hudson's Bay supply steamer Northcote to be converted into a gunboat. Boxes, chests, mattresses, planks, sandbags and sacks of grain were used as armor for troops aboard. Armed with one 7-pounder cannon, one Gatling gun and about 35 militiamen, the flat-bottomed steamer was supposed to attack Batoche from the river at the same time that the militia launched their land assault. Hoping to surprise the Metis defenders in a deadly crossfire, Middleton planned that the Northcote would steam down the river past Batoche and disembark the militia who would attack the Metis from the riverside as his army moved into the village.

In Batoche fear had begun to be experienced by the defenders. All the elderly, woman and children stayed in their huts and only emerged reluctantly when Riel would summon them to hear any news or his hopeful prophecies of the upcoming conflict's result. So far the news had been very good and hopeful: three battles with three victories accomplished. But when Riel and Gabriel Dumont looked into the faces of the people, stiff with fear, they knew that they were not deceived. But he also knew, and was confident in his Metis fighter's bravery and skilled marksmanship he would put up against any Canadian military force, militia or regular army.

Louis harangued his people. If he should be killed, he said, they need not cry or mourn for him. He would return from the grave and prove his divine mission in life. "Look!" Louis said to them. "Look at those devils trying to murder our nation by savage soldiers paid by your own Government to destroy the half-breed nation! To arms! Or will you crouch and meekly just submit? Our God tells you to follow me; the Holy Ghost is with you in my person. Courage! We will conquer them!"

The people obeyed their orders mutely, went about the business assigned to them by Gabriel and his captains, and their attitude and expressions told their chiefs that the war would be lost. When the warriors returned to their cabins for their meals they would usually find the women weeping and rebuking them for this unwanted and frightful war.

As Middleton's half-frozen militia trudged through snow and

icy roads northward, Louis Riel's Provisional Government of Saskatchewan met daily, opening its sessions with a prayer that Riel had composed for them: O Lord, our God, who art the Father of mercy and consolation, we are several French-Canadian Metis gathered together in council, who put our confidence in thee; grant that we may not be covered with confusion, ever defend us from this, enlighten us in our darkness of doubt, encourage us in our trials, strengthen us all in our weaknesses, and succor us in this disturbing time of pressing need,

But Gabriel Dumont would chafe at such pious pastimes. He should be in the field. His scouts had intercepted telegrams reporting the Canadian's movements and he had a spy with them. As an aggressive, confident warrior and tactician he knew that if he could convince Riel to allow his men to pursue his guerilla-like methods that they could possibly force a stalemate with Middleton's army and induce the Canadian Government to negotiate with Riel.

This enabled Dumont to know every movement of the troops. Now he felt was the best time to launch a guerilla campaign, he told Riel, which would hold up Middleton's advance and attack for weeks, even months. His plan was completely sound strategically. He would disrupt the Canadians transport and military supplies of ammunition and food by dynamiting the Canadian Pacific Railway tracks in multiple places and also make sudden and unexpected incursions on the lightly-protected prairie outposts where food for the troops and hay for the horse would be stored. He also planned to worry and demoralize the Canadians by hurling swift nightly raids on their foolishly exposed or lightly manned positions along their route north. Dumont knew that the Canadian's would be exhausted after their long, snow-covered march north. Later, Dumont commented that if he had been permitted to implement this plan, "I could have made the soldiers so edgy that at the end of three nights they would have been at each other's throats."

But Riel refused to accept Dumont's guerilla warfare plans as he still hoped that the Metis outbursts would be regarded as a demonstration and a threat and all avenues to peace still open. The

Metis have friends among the advancing troops, Riel insisted. This caused Gabriel to scoff, "I wouldn't consider as our friends those who would join the English to kill and plunder us." "If you knew them," Louis responded, "you wouldn't try to treat them that way." Besides, he felt Gabriel's tactics were "too much like some inhumane tactics of the Indians." Gabriel had reached the end of his patience; his love and respect for Riel kept him from acting.

"I have seen a flock of dark geese," Riel once brooded in the journal he was keeping at Batoche. "They had the appearance of wandering away, but in truth they were hovering in the air. I then saw them disperse into two groups...one group had flown east   - though they were not in the sunshine, they did not reflect the light; they were covered in darkness." Riel was worried that the Metis not fragment and disperse like the geese. This troubling thought was another reason for his not wanting to agree to Dumont's guerilla campaign. This lack of tactical acumen, and the fear that if the Metis were dispersed in any manner, it would prove a big disadvantage against a regular army having superior manpower and unlimited armament and supplies.

Canada's Northwest field force was on the move north. They had to undergo a two hundred and thirty mile march from the railhead at Qu'Appelle to Batoche. Much farther west, Major General T. Bland Strange was marching through Alberta toward Edmonton with six hundred men to forestall the Blackfeet from going back on their promise to remain neutral if a rebellion were to surface.

The Metis forces had by now lost their best opportunity to interfere with the Government's war machine with Dumont's suggested tactics. It was too late to dynamite the railroad, also too late to attack the detraining depots, largely because of Riel's disagreement with Dumont more than three thousand Government forces, widely dispersed, had reached the Northwest Territories safely, and were now marching against the Metis rebels. Dumont could only rely on 500 Metis for defense.

Dumont's major concern was Middleton's force marching toward Batoche. It still might be possible to sack the supply depots on the prairie and harass troops and transport. The Canadians were floundering north on crude prairie trails with horses slipping and stumbling.

At times their mounts stumbled to their knees on hard-packed snow or icy ruts in the road, the next moment they would plunge to their bellies in quicksand or in mud. The transport wagons, carts and guns were often mired in marshy creek bottoms. Alkali emerged out of the sod to poison drinking water, burn into the horse's hooves acid-like, and even eat into the leather of the trooper's boots. Moisture and icy cold worked through the troopers uniforms which were being worn out on their long trek from Lake Superior. The first night out of Qu'Appelle the temperature was twenty-three below zero. The next morning the tent pegs had to be chopped out of the ground with axes.

Jerome Henry, a teamster with Middleton's forces and a Metis spy, made it clear that transport could be a very vulnerable aspect of the campaign. Four hundred horses were the minimum needed to move the column's supplies, and it was impossible to guard that many horses on the open prairie. But even these were not enough forcing Middleton to order additional supplies, especially feed for the horses.

The steamer Northcote, slowly forcing its way through drifting ice, grounding on sand bars became late for its appointed rendezvous with Middleton's force. Gen. Middleton waited impatiently for days then finally decided to press on. He also unwisely, decided to split his forces so as to be able to launch a two-prong attack on the Batoche village. Forming up two columns of almost equal strength, he had them start north along both banks of the South Saskatchewan River. A map of the Canadian's position at Clarke's Crossing and information about Middleton's plan of the march, soon reached Gabriel Dumont through his alert spies, and the Metis General knew he had a last opportunity to possibly do a wrecking job on Middleton's offensive program.

Dumont realized that he had enough fighters and ammunition to engage only half of Middleton's army, but if he waited he would be compelled to try to defend a fixed position against far superior forces. The Metis fighting forte as was their Indian allies was basically as cavalrymen and guerillas. Both were in fighting temperament unsuited to withstand siege warfare, and additionally could they gather enough food and ammunition for such an ordeal.

Foolishly acting against the advice of men familiar with the prairie terrain and the enemy's likely tactics, Middleton left most of his cavalry behind to guard the rail depots and the vulnerable rear of his division when the cavalry should have been employed in the van. Some settlers, all experienced riders and marksmen volunteered to patrol the railway and boundary, which would have released man y of his men; he ignored the offer, but they organized anyway. His most serious error, which was one that falsely gave rise to unjustified charges, spread across Canada by newspaper correspondents and returning militiamen, that the Northwest Mounted Police were cowards and that they had shirked a fair share of combat.

The troops with Middleton and the newspaper correspondents were unaware of all this, and the derisive nickname "gophers" was applied to the Mounties, un-deservedly.as they had been chafing in the enforced confinement by Gen. Middleton. Nothing could have been more unjust to the most courageous and most intelligent group of whites in the country. Their Major, Sam Steele and a small detachment, at great risk of their lives, captured a Metis spy from the camp of Chief Crowfoot, head of the Blackfeet, jailing him, helping to persuade the most dangerous warriors to keep out of conflict.

In the afternoon of May 7th the Canadian force halted at Gabriel's Crossing, camped and the steamer Northcote tied up. Using timbers brought from Dumont's stables at the crossing, the lower deck was rimmed all around with a double wall of two-inch planks. Sacks of oats and other material were packed on the upper deck and around the vulnerable pilothouse. The ship's armament consisted of one small cannon, the lone Gatling gun and the trooper's rifle. Civilian Captains Seager and Sheets and Purser Talbot, all took a dim view of the entire project, but they had no choice. The Northcote, dragging clumsy barges was to head downstream to Batoche, then await Middleton's ground force to arrive, then open fire upon Riel's stronghold from the river, timed to coincide with the ground troops attacking on land. If Dumont and his fighters had allowed this to happen, they would be trapped between two broad-sides of fire, probably ending the war there and then. The Metis were not likely to cooperate as they had scouts posted watching the enemy's operation and their "armor-plating" of the Northcote, then reporting the details to Dumont.

A set of signals was in place so that the Northcote could communicate with the land forces. by whistle. The land force would reply with bugle calls. After all was ready, Captains Seager and Sheets who doubled as the ship's pilots, still had troubling doubts; only the lower section of the pilothouse was protected so their vision wouldn't be obstructed. Now, early morning of May 7th they tooted the whistle, answered by a bugle from the ranks of Canadians ashore.

At the Metis stronghold of Batoche, Gabriel Dumont was busy. He directed dozens of well concealed rifle pits, reinforced with mounds of earth and heavy logs. The rifle pits were positioned atop inclines dug in at critical points along the trail and in heavily wooded areas. He also had pits hollowed out around narrow bridges over the many creeks flowing near the village, as well as on high banks on both sides of the river and at the crest of a slope above the village. When completed, the defenses were manned by some 350 Metis and a small group of Indians. Only 200 to 250 of Dumont's forces were equipped with rifles, muzzleloaders and their hunting shotguns.

Moving slowly to join Dumont's warriors – but too slowly to get there in time to contribute to the defenses – were an unknown number of Metis reinforcements, probably not more than fifty, and Chief Poundmaker's Crees.

When the Canadian's march resumed the morning of May 8th, the troops took a wide detour over a prairie trail which would take them several miles from the river and bring them back to Batoche village from the east. The Northcote's Captains were ordered to remain where they were for the day, and then to proceed cautiously the next morning.

The plan was for the steamer and troops to meet at Batoche the morning of May 9th at nine o'clock. General Middleton the most cautious a commander one could imagine, had done everything he could devise to build an overwhelming attack plan, except one aspect of his plan would have been to employ the experienced Northwest Mounted Police at Prince Albert. Should everything have gone as Middleton planned, the last stronghold of Riel's New Metis Nation of the west, the log-cabin capitol of this half-breed race would fall at most in a few hours. Meanwhile, at Batoche, the most indomitable man that the New Nation of the Metis were fortunate to have as military commander, Gabriel Dumont, continued his careful preparations. He now had to face and to plan for a battle of position he had tried to avoid, and would have avoided, but for Louis Riel's overruling Dumont's plan and plea for guerilla warfare.

Dumont examined and checked over the Metis assets and tactical liabilities. He had two hundred plus fighters, everyone a sharpshooter due to their many years of hunting buffalo and other game. The few cowards who had fled from the Fish Creek conflict were weeded out. His fighters were armed with a variety of weapons; Springfield, Winchester and Martini-Henry rifles; many shotguns and ancient muzzle-loaders. That was a handicap compared to their enemy's superior armament. But he knew that it couldn't be helped; he had to play the cards he was dealt.

As to the terrain, Gabriel and his fighters knew every inch, every hole in the ground and brush and logs to take cover behind. They also were endowed with a psychological benefit: a prophet in Louis Riel, with a wonder-working voice, some encouraging letters from a Bishop and a crucifix a foot and a half long. Well, but was this enough to overcome the numerical odds? He had always known they couldn't win against the power and resources of the Dominion in Ottawa. The most troublesome factor to Dumont was that his warriors would be terribly short of ammunition. He constantly reminded them to "make every shot you fire, count!"

Chapter 9
STRENGTH VS. VALOR

Saturday, May 9, 1885

Dawn came at four o'clock. At five thirty the Northwest Field Force was on the march nine miles east of Batoche. Seventy five mounted scouts led, under the command of Major Boulton who had once was under a possible sentencing in the Fort Garry rebellion. Following was the Gatling gun on its wheeled carriage, along with other guns.

At seven o'clock the steamer Northcote cast off lines and started down river from Clarke's Crossing. It had been under way for less than an hour. It was nearing a long sand bar which jutted out into the river from the eastern shore, near the southern edge of the Batoche spread out settlements. The channel being very narrow at this point, the boat's pilot was feeling his way, close to the brush-covered bank opposite the sand bar.

Suddenly, with no visible or verbal signal, rifle and shotgun fire from both banks of the river raked the boat's decks. With no support from the land force, it became an easy target when Metis spotted the craft. The voluminous shooting came from well camouflaged trenches and rifle pits. All of that heavy fusillade however, used up much of the Metis' precious ammunition that they would be in need of in the fighting to follow.

Bullets hit harmlessly into the heavy, thick timbers behind which the troopers lay prone, but the bullets pierced the thin walls of the upper deck. There, sick men rolled out of their bunks in the cabin thrusting mattresses against the walls. Lieutenant Macdonald, the Canadian Prime Ministers son, his face swollen and aflame from his malady, seized a rifle and crawled out on deck.

Dumont, standing in the stirrups of his horse came out to the riverbank. He shouted orders to the Metis marksmen for the line of fire to move higher. As their bullets riddled the pilot house, the helmsman, with wood splinters everywhere and a bullet hole in his jacket, released the wheel and dropped prone to the floor.

Now out of control, the Northcote careened into the sand bar, caught in the current, brushed against the other side of the channel. Dumont shouted again and a few Metis broke from cover, running to try and board the lurching vessel, but the Gatling gun opened up on them and they raced back. Gabriel watched for a moment, ignoring the bullets flying around him; then as he saw that the current would keep the boat from grounding, he spurred his horse setting off in a run for the center of the settlement.

It was now eight o'clock, an hour before Gen. Middleton had scheduled the beginning of the Batoche battle, and the troops were nearly four miles away. The boat's purser, Talbot, with his rifle in hand, crawled into the bullet-raked pilot house to "cover" the helmsman, Captain Seager, who had been able to take the ship's wheel again and now had the steamer under control and straightened out.

Co-Captain Sheets and the engine crew were building steam pressure to the limit; Seager swung the boat into the middle of the river as the Northcote ran for its life. Only one or two shells were fired from its cannon; the gun was too slow. But the Gatling gun raked the banks behind the boat keeping the Metis at a distance.

The steamer reached the center of the settlement and headed for the ferry landing. Too late, Captain Seager saw Dumont and a group of Metis working feverishly with the two ferry cables. He tried to stop the boat, but its momentum carried it on as the Metis dropped one of the cables to the river's surface, just behind his vessel. The other cable, a few feet ahead, was coming down also. Seager signaled frantically for full speed ahead, plowed into the cable just as it scraped the top of the pilot house. The Northcote's two stacks, its mast, its two tall spars and its whistle were yanked off, flung on the upper deck. The deck began to immediately burn.

While a bucket brigade dowsed the deck under fire, the vessel slid around the big bend in the river. The Metis firing dropped off;

the steamer was out of range now and almost safe. Captain Seager went on another mile or two and dropped anchor in mid-channel. All hands went to work to repair the torn and charred deck and reset the stacks, spar and mast. Restoring the ship's whistle on its high position on a stack was the most dangerous job and no one would volunteer until Private C. Coombes of the Toronto Infantry School Corps, promised fifty dollars volunteered. Just as he finished a Metis sniper spotted him and opened fire, too late.

Bedson and others tried to induce the ship's civilian Captain and crew to swing about and go back to Batoche, but they all refused. They argued, rightly so, that the Northcote was not a gunboat. Three men had been wounded while the rickety craft ran the gauntlet of fire for five miles. If they did return they would not be able to get past the lowered ferry cables and they would all be sitting ducks.

The Canadian military had to finally admit that the civilian Captain was right. So the first ship converted into a "warship" on the western prairies became non-combatants for the balance of the Batoche conflict. The Metis fighters were now between the Northcote and the advancing army; soon everyone was too busy to be concerned about it.

The last scattered firing at the Northcote ceased, when, right at nine o'clock, Middleton's two columns advanced, one on each side of the river. Advance guards could now see the Church of St. Antoine and its parish house. Behind the buildings and continuing for quite a distance to the north, the troops could see dense thickets of willow brush and small poplar trees, perfect cover for Dumont's expert riflemen and snipers.

The Batoche village proper lay in a ravine below, and not yet visible to the marching troops. Across the road from the church on a small hill above the river valley was the cemetery; near it were a few small cabins, the usual Metis homes. Gen. Middleton allowed no preliminaries or delay for parleys and negotiating. He was in no mood for delays of any sort. The Gatling gun escorted by Boulton's scouts, was rushed to the forefront, unlimbered and directed to fire at the few cabins near the Metis cemetery. The gunner then began raking their thick, log walls. The battle for Batoche began.

A few elderly men, along with some women and children who were non-combatants, and who had remained near the church to avoid any involvement in the fighting, rushed from the cabins, through the brush and down into a ravine seeking some form of shelter and safety. Apparently with the cabins now empty, the advancing soldiers faced no returning fire.

Soon, more and more troops arrived, and dropping to their knees, began firing over the crest of a small hill to persuade any Metis to keep their distance while the heavy-firing Gatling gun was now moved forward to between the church and cemetery.

Suddenly a white handkerchief appeared at the church's door. Middleton had his men cease firing while he and some staff began conversing with the parish priests. At this parley, or possible another, the Metis forces were betrayed. Despite their denials, it surfaced later that there was little doubt that the priests were angry at Riel's apostasy and disclosed to Middleton as much of the Metis battle plans, and, of more importance, revealed that the Metis were sorely short of food and ammunition.

Against the testimony of the priests, their perfidy and betrayal even after a written pledge, was declared by Metis veterans and Gabriel Dumont. In addition, accounts written during the battle by Canadian officers, volunteers and newspapermen validated their charges. One militiaman wrote, "A quarter of an hour was spent in Middleton's conference with the priests, from whom it was learned that Dumont's fighters numbered about two hundred half-breeds and as many Indians. This estimate was far too high, as the Indians – Chief Poundmaker's – had not arrived. Also, the Metis force was equally divided by the river and were completely without flour, sugar, tea, and especially short on ammunition, especially lead." Also the priests divulged that some of the Metis had begun to be somewhat dissatisfied with Riel and his increased negative opinions of the church.

Many Metis survivors of their definitive conflict often would complain that they were defeated by the treachery of the priests, and some so bitter that they never became reconciled to the

Church.

As a sad result of his church's betrayal, Gabriel Dumont hated the clergy to the end of his life and never ceased to work to nullify its influence with his people. "We learned," years later Dumont said from a reliable source that though Middleton had reinforcements despaired of defeating us, notwithstanding that some traitors advised him that we were almost out of ammunition, and apart from a few, all the Metis fighters were discouraged. And besides if Middleton's forces didn't hurry, Indians would arrive to reinforce us." Who cannot fully understand and commiserate with Gabriel Dumont and his life-long bitterness and hatred for their deceitful clergy. The time-frame in the Batoche assault was so critical in that if Middleton was not informed of reinforcements in the form of Chief Poundmaker's hundreds of warriors he would not have moved as quickly in the assault of the village.

As the troops had advanced as far as the church without encountering any resistance, the priests, nuns and a few Metis who had sought refuge with them appeared to be safe in the parish house as anywhere, and remained there.

Meanwhile, Middleton's cannon began to shell the village proper. Some shot struck the Walter and Baker store and house several times, causing fires which didn't spread. Some of the Metis regarded this as a miracle attributed to the flag they had raised over the house. It was a makeshift cotton banner to which a paper portrait of the Virgin Mary. The house used by the Metis Council for its meetings, which bore a flag with a portrait of Christ also was struck but was not destroyed.

Occasionally the shelling would bring out a few noncombatants. Nor a single Metis had yet to become visible to the troopers. This unusual development encouraged the Canadians to move forward beyond the church, with the Gatling gun in the front rank as usual. Even this continuing forward movement by the troops still did not cause any Metis to become visible to them.

Suddenly, less than thirty yards in front of the leading army, firing began to rise in burst from the steep, sloping hillside right in their faces. The foremost ranks stood, surprised and gazing at the deadly puffs of smoke. They appeared to coming right out of the ground itself, with no notice of any Metis warrior doing the shooting. Panic seized the soldiers and they turned and fled.

Their officers ordered the guns to be pulled back; one of them, caught in the thick brush, could not be loosened immediately and its frightened and demoralized crew would have abandoned it when Howard, the American Gatling enthusiast and proponent, who had made no move to retreat with his Gatling, silenced the Metis firing in the gun's area. By keeping up a constant fusillade of rapid fire bullets, he was able to hold back the rebels while the gun was withdrawn. Now alone, as the gunner beside him lay moaning, shot through both legs – the Connecticut American held the line for their retreat. Only after the Canadians had reformed back at the church did gunner Howard pull back his Gatling.

The Canadian officers now discovered what they were up against. The terrain to their front was honeycombed with concealed, camouflaged rifle pits, even superior to the ones at Fish Creek. Not only the banks of the ravine, but the meadow below it between the hill and the river held rifle pits every few yards and, they extended for almost a mile in depth. These defensive preparations covered over a front of over a mile and a half, from beyond the cemetery to the south to several hundred yards back of the church to the north. The Canadian commanders eventually discovered that the death-dealing rifle pits ranged in size from holes barely large enough for one man, to elaborate trenches accommodating up to a dozen deadly riflemen.

These trenches usually held a dozen loop holed logs, carefully and skillfully camouflaged with dirt and brush, set at the edge of the trench facing the enemy. Down in the meadow, behind the hillside rifle pits, Gabriel Dumont rested on one knee with his Winchester aimed at the skyline. As he called out orders to the nearest pits, from man-to-man they were relayed up the bank to the men in the most forward positions.

Metis crept from their pits, crawling on their bellies up the slope in communication trenches covered with brush. Their earthen-colored clothing blended in the terrain perfectly; even had the Canadian scouts had dared to expose themselves by peeking over the hilltop, they probably would not have detected the movements. Previously prepared rifle pits at the edge of the cemetery and in the heavy brush behind the church, on the left flanks of the Canadian column were silently occupied.

The rebels now mounted a new attack from the left, but most of the Metis on that flank happened to be armed with shotguns, and their fire fell short. The Canadians thus were able to hold their ground but could not effectively reply, even with the aid of the Gatling, because as before the enemy was invisible. When a more effective Metis fusillade started on the right flank, it almost trapped a battery causing another withdrawal to be ordered by Canadian officers. The first wounded Canadians had been placed in the church; they were now removed and evacuated to the rear.

A sinister crackling and a sudden hot wind alerted Middleton's force that the Metis had once again resorted to a favorite ploy; they had fired the brush and grass on both sides of the militia column. Soon a dense cloud of acrid smoke began to roll over the prairie. Remembering this experience in the Fish Creek conflict, the Canadians and militiamen became uneasy and fell back somewhat.

The nervous troops their eyes smarting from the intrusive smoke, tried to see the enemy through the murkiness and saw none, but they saw comrades in their solid line, shelter less on the open prairie being methodically picked off. Howard was grimly firing the Gatling gun into the smoke, with no idea of targets or of range. His intent, probably successful, was to prevent a Metis charge.

It was now one o'clock in that first afternoon. Having only advanced a short distance to the church, but driven back by Dumont's marksman and his strategic ability they fell back again were not to get that far again for three more days.

With their advantage of complete concealment, the Metis, the Canadian command feared, could hold out indefinitely if they had food and ammunition aplenty. The priests having told them that they lacked these essentials, it was hoped that the priests were correct, and could be trusted. But could they? Otherwise it was acknowledged sadly, "one rebel is as good as ten volunteers."

Middleton then ordered an improvised stockade, erected a few hundred yards east of the church and directed that all of the field force's animals and equipment be brought up from the overnight camp. In mid afternoon Lord Melgud, the representative of the Governor General and Middleton's chief of staff, left suddenly, headed back to Ottawa. This event led to the rumor that Middleton was appealing for British regulars, but in actuality Lord Melgud had left on private matters.

The Canadians made one or two more sorties toward the cemetery as the smoke cleared but were easily driven off by Dumont's entrenched sharpshooters. The last few hours of daylight featured only desultory firing from either side. The Metis were obviously conserving their ammunitions.

Chapter 10
MAY TENTH: STALEMATE

At sunset the Canadians withdrew to the stockade, to the accompaniment of jeers and singing from the Metis positions. After the Gatling gun had also pulled back, snipers cautiously trailed the Canadians. Howard's entry into the camp brought loud cheering, as the volunteers knew that he and his deadly Gatling had saved their advance echelon from possible destruction. The short range of the rebels' ammunition kept them at a safe distance as their gunfire would not reach the Gatling and beyond. Howard brought with him to the stockade a souvenir: an ivory-handled knife he had taken from a dead Indian. It had been a United States cavalry saber, shortened and shaped by the Sioux brave from whose body he had recovered it.

A shaded candle in the hospital tent was the only light allowed in the stockade. As no fires were permitted, their dinner was hardtack and water. General Middleton himself had to retire in a darkened tent. After the men rolled up in their blankets for the night, the nerve-war tactics that Dumont had wanted use weeks before began to be employed by the Metis: an intermittent rain of bullets and other missiles fell into the compound, keeping the soldiers awake and on edge and frightening the hundreds of animals sharing the very limited space. Some troopers took shelter under the wagons, but many had to walk with the horsed all night to prevent the horses from stampeding and causing trooper injuries.

The stockade had been poorly located, fully exposed on the side of a slight rise in the prairie without brush or trees for shelter. Unaccountably it had been placed in a plowed field, and the men and animals stumbled about in choking dust which obscured what little starlight was able to be seen.

Metis sporadic firing continued sporadically through the night, causing few casualties but kept the troops awake. At midnight a huge rocket burst over the stockade and for a few moments it was brightly illuminated. Startled from their fitful sleep, the Canadians bumped their heads on the wagon beds, swearing; They rolled out of their blankets but soon crawled back as bullets, buckshot and scrap metal rained down on them. No one was wounded, though a few of the horses were hit; but they had another puzzle to keep them awake: Where in earth had the ill-armed Metis forces managed to obtain the huge flare?

SUNDAY

A film of ice had formed on their water pails and the troops were stiff and sore when they were called awake at four a.m. Derisive shouts and challenges and some scattered shooting from the Metis greeted them at their first stirring and activity.

Skirmish lines were sent out at five-thirty and their guns were again pushed forward until the crews came in sight of the village. Employing a steady cannonading, most of the housed were soon reduced to rubble. One of the most seriously damaged was the big "Batoche House" in the cellar of which a dozen whites had been imprisoned along with one Metis recalcitrant, Albert Monkman, formerly a member of Riel's Council. The others were a disparate group; telegraph maintenance men, freighters, storekeepers, or captured Canadian scouts for the most part; but included were Riel's former secretary and his brother, who had come from Prince Albert to find him. Middleton's cannon, firing nine-pound shells, could not be traversed low enough on their fixed carriages to bombard the rifle pits on the sloping hillside; the shrapnel shells would burst harmlessly in the trees overhead or far beyond the entrenchments. Meanwhile the Metis fighters were conserving their ammunition and fired less frequently than they had the preceding day. The Canadian's Midland Battalion, taking a lesson from their opponents, dug its own foxholes and was able to hold its position all day without loss. For the first time some effort was also made to provide some protection and concealment for their cannon and the Gatling.

The militia had been ordered on leaving the camp that morning to avoid reckless gestures or foolish movements. General Middleton had decided to devote the day primarily to artillery action and, by destroying the Batoche village to affect the Metis morale – counting upon the assurances of the Metis priests that the rebels could not withstand a siege for very long. His troops did not get within two hundred yards of their furthermost advance of the day, and there were in fact, hours when there was no firing from rifles. Middleton once, while walking among the guns with a cane under his arm, was startled by an unexpected burst of rifle fire from his troop. "Hold your fire", he yelled." "What on earth are you shooting at?" The, under his breath, he grumbled, "Damned fools!" A Canadian officer hearing the remarks, flushed red with resentment.

Middleton insisted, when conferring with his staff that he did not have enough men to take Batoche by storm. He had entered the field of combat with nine-hundred and seventeen men under arms, almost five times the rebels manpower; but throughout the campaign he would overestimate the enemy and prefer to act cautiously, insisting later that he wished to keep casualties at a minimum.

In addition, during his conversations with the Metis priests he was inclined to accept inaccurate Metis manpower figures without any effort to confirm them by not employing any espionage. On Sunday afternoon, his Grenadiers were ordered to attempt a feint – a sudden attack, then a faked headlong retreat. This, it was hoped, might draw the Metis from their rifle pits and entrenchments and into a position which had been secretly occupied by the Canadian Ninetieth Battalion.

But their planned maneuver failed; a few nervous and trigger-happy riflemen of the Ninetieth opened fire too soon and by doing so betrayed their waiting positions. So the metis held in their dugouts. Gabriel Dumont again spent hours kneeling in the meadow, out of range of the Canadians unless they came over the hill. Behind and before him, clutching his big, foot-and-a-half crucifix, Louis Riel moved about the Metis positions in the rifle pits, exhorting them to keep up their courage for the glory of God. Every day at dawn he would also lead the fighters and their families in prayers in a grove down by the river.

At six o'clock the Canadian forces again began to fall back to the stockade, Dumont's fighters, taking advantage of the fact that the sun was in the eyes of the troops, darted over the crest of the ravine to harass the departing troops and the first important skirmish of the day started in the field before the church. But the Canadians, without shelter, could not make a stand; again, the most-valuable Gatling gun had to cover the withdrawal. Meanwhile, in the stockade, the chaplain was starting funeral services for a gunner killed the day before. While he was engaged two more were killed. This caused the Canadians further nervousness as they realized that they were still vulnerable to the Metis marksman even in a sheltered position.

The last of Middleton's transport contingent had arrived from the camp nine miles east and its wagons were used to help strengthen the stockade's protection for the men who would sleep underneath the wagon's bed for safety. Several detachments had also been assigned to build earthworks surrounding their encampment. This allowed the troops to retire that night to a much improved and stronger position than they had the previous night. They also were able to get some sleep because the Metis, under Dumont's directives, chose not to waste their dwindling ammunition on their "nerve war." The troops now found it even safe to light fires, and the Canadian's at last were able to enjoy a hot meal and tea.

For the most part the troops were angry. General Middleton's decision to win the conflict by siege methods was highly unpopular. They felt that this method of fighting reflected negatively on their courage. Also the occasional indecisive skirmishing and the discomfort of the nights in the stockade were harder on the whites than on the Metis. Again the cry arose from the rank and file: let's get on with it and end it, now!

Meanwhile at the Metis camp, Middleton's over-cautiousness and timidity had served to give Gabriel Dumont and Louis Riel some new hope. They had held off and foiled the Canadian's much larger force for two days now, which invigorated their élan. More messengers raced off to Chief Poundmaker's camp, imploring him to hurry. They felt that with the aid of Poundmaker's warriors it would greatly enable Batoche to hold out two or three days longer giving the defenders a chance – the slimmest of chances – that the invaders could be routed and Batoche saved.

But in Chief Poundmaker's camp discussions and arguments, pro and con re: moving out to Batoche's aid were time-consuming. The ongoing arguments and opinions absorbed the energies of the Crees. There were pro-war parties and peace parties and traditionally their democratic system concerning major decisions allowed all parties respectful attention while they pleaded their cause and opinions. Poundmaker, who had made peace with the Blackfeet and was known from the Mackenzie to the Missouri Rivers as a great chief, was an internationalist. He had always been friendly with the whites, and was temperamentally inclined to peace and to avoid war.

Finally, he took a realistic position: could the Indians and Metis forces, even when combined, win? They couldn't he told his council of chiefs, because "Riel has too little powder and cartridge." How he had been able to learn this salient fact is a mystery. The Metis messengers to his camp would have been careful not to betray any Batoche weaknesses to him. There were day-long debates about the trustworthiness and fighting abilities of Riel's Metis and his ally Big Bear. Riel's urgent letters, translated from French into Cree, by Riel's envoys, were read and re-read looking for possible hidden meanings or true disclosures of the Metis situation and capabilities.

Finally there was talk about honor. The Crees had accepted and smoked the peace-pipe tobacco Gabriel Dumont had sent; they were pledged. Then, because no Indian could speak against the honor of their band, the tipis were struck and the camp began moving east toward Batoche. Democracy was at work, helping to defeat itself. Unfortunately for Louis Riel, Gabriel Dumont and their fighting men, even if the Cree's long-winded discussions had been shortened for just one day, it could have made a big difference in the battle's outcome. It would also be another what-if memory to plague Gabriel Dumont for years.

Chapter 11
FINALE

Middleton spent most of May 11th in reconnaissance looking for ways and methods to launch a major, decisive attack. The Metis cleverly had moved overnight to other hidden rifle pits and trenches, so periodically whenever the Canadian ranks would move to take their previously defensive positions, they would suddenly find themselves under fire from new, almost unseen locations.

In Batoche, Dumont moved continuously among his follower's rifle pits, constantly sending his defense orders as he stressed his overarching need;" hold your fire until you're absolutely sure of your target, we must save our ammunition!" Gabriel was led to believe that General Middleton had almost sixteen hundred men at his command and couldn't fathom the Canadian's reluctance to make a major assault with such a superiority of men, guns and ammunition. But he took advantage of their failure to attack by continually moving his fighters rapidly and secretly over their wide front and spreading their meager fire. Dumont's tactics had convinced Middleton that the priests estimates of Riel's forces and strength, had been if anything, very low.

In Batoche's ruined council hut, Riel wrote prophesies in his "Commonplace Book" and devised new prayers. In caves they had dug into the riverbanks on both sides of the stream, the women and children huddled together awaiting the end of the Metis turmoil and battle outcome. Riel was still carrying about his long crucifix, encouraging and calming their fears as best as he could. The noncombatants were sleeping on straw and subsisting meagerly on the last of their foodstuff.

Some were forced to eat horse and dog meat. Dumont sent out

hunters, most of them their Indian comrades-in-arms to range about the prairie on the west side seeking stray cattle which they drove back to the river and butchered.

The priests and nuns, most of them convinced that they were doomed, prayed incessantly for grace, courage and God's aid in their trials. The parish house was now in the center of the battlefield, but there were no accommodations for them in the Canadian's stockade, nor would they have been much safer there. Safety lay west of the river, but to get there they would have to go through the Metis lines – and Gabriel Dumont, for one, probably not hesitated to shoot the disloyal priests on sight.

The religious contingent did not escape unscratched. Early Monday evening father Moulin went to the attic of the parish house on some errand and in passing an open window was struck by a bullet from a Metis rifle. The shot had not been aimed at him and the bullet's force was spent; he received a painful but not serious flesh wound to his head. His people signaled with an improvised red flag, firing stopped and the wounded missionary was taken on a Canadian stretcher to the hospital tent in the army's corral.

Monday turned out to be a fruitless repetition of the preceding day; nothing happened on the battlefield except that the Canadian's were shifted and new units given a taste of Dumont's Metis marksmanship. At sunset the troops again retired to the crowded, stinking stockade where the dust and manure were now ankle-deep. The troops were complaining in many cases of their commanding officers putting them through the worrisome and disgusting nightly retirement to the stockade. Some felt they would rather attack and get the lagging battle over with,

Frustrated by continuing inaction, Middleton's officers approached him with demands that a general offensive be planned for the next day. Even Howard, more and more impatient, begged for permission to go forward alone with his Gatling gun and clear out the first row of rifle pits.

Middleton would not agree to an all-out charge, but he did agree to outline new and more aggressive tactics which he was willing to try. Word spread through the camp upon hearing of the news that tomorrow might end the militia's discouraging ordeal.

Early that morning, May 12th, Louis Riel told his people gathered in the grove that this could be the day which would decide the fate of the Metis race His prophetic vision had disclosed, he said, that if the skies were clear, their village would survive, but if it happened that clouds gathered and obscured the sun that the Metis cause would be doomed.

The women, children and Metis elders gazed overhead, wide-eyed; the men fidgeting with their guns, glanced covertly at the horizon, at the hot, blazing sun beginning to appear in the east. There was not even a wisp of cloud appearing in the clear, blue heavens above. The women gave thanks and gratefully murmured their response to Riel's Prayers. The elders and men laughed and began to joke among themselves. It would be a good day all thought.

General Middleton, with about 150 of his militia including a small cavalry detachment, the Gatling gun and one cannon, set out in the morning on a wide sweep around the northeast flank of the rebel's positions. He was attempting to create a diversion, under cover of which the main infantry force would attack the Metis center, where the heaviest concentration of their deadly riflemen commanded the best route into the ravine.

In midmorning Middleton's cannon was heard, but it fired only two or three times and there was no sound of firing by his riflemen. Lt. Col. Van Straubenzie, commanding the center ranks of Canadian's, concluded that something had gone wrong and did not order his troops to advance.

At noon Middleton and his proposed diversionary force returned – the General, according to eyewitnesses, "In a towering rage" because his orders had not been obeyed stymieing his overall attack plans. In vain his staff protested that a few shots from his cannon – without any rifle fire accompanying it, couldn't be thought of by Van Straubenzie to be the diversion planned.

Nevertheless Middleton's strategy had turned out to be worthwhile. The dug-in rebels after three days of successful resistance on a comparatively narrow frontage, were alarmed and puzzled by the enemy's movement, abortive as it was, and fell into the trap by strengthening that flank of their line at the expense of their center. In addition General Middleton now had some evidence of weakening resolution among the Metis: a message from Riel. John W. Astley, a surveyor and one of the prisoners at Batoche, mounted and carrying a white flag, had brought it through the lines to Middleton that morning. Riel's message read: "if you massacre our families, we are going to massacre the Indian agent and other prisoners." Middleton sent Astley back with a polite reply: "Mr. Riel, I am anxious to avoid killing or injuring any women or children and have done my best to avoid doing so. Put your women and children together in one safe place, and let me know where it is and no shot shall be fired into their area. I trust to your honor not to put men with them." Astley immediately left the camp with instructions to deliver the message - only to Louis Riel.

But neither the General himself, nor the force he had left behind, had taken advantage of the morning's opportunity for any gains. At noon he had lunch grumpily in the stockade. He ordered the troops to take up their static positions of the day before: at the extreme left, toward the cemetery, the Midland Battalion of Port Hope, Ontario, commanded by Lt. Col. Williams, with Captain John French's company of scouts; left center, the Royal Grenadiers of Toronto. Lt. Col. H.J. Grassett; right center, Ninetieth Battalion Rifles of Winnipeg, Lt. Col. McKeand; extreme right, Boulton's and Dennis' scouts, and Howard with his Gatling gun.

This was the Canadians usual skirmishing position, from which brief and ineffective sorties had been made by various units for the past three days. But finally, at least one of Middleton's officers, Lt. Col. Williams of the Midland Battalion, had had a bellyful of caution. Williams was the son of a British Naval officer and was himself a member of the Dominion Parliament. Soon he would be ordered to move forward cautiously, as before, feel out the Metis strength, and then retire; but from man to man the word spread that when the order came, Col. Williams and his Midland force would keep on going. Quickly the whispers came back from the

Grenadiers and the Ninetieth, promising their support.

For the first time since Saturday the skirmishers were able to reach the church, and General Middleton established his command headquarters there. Then the Midland Battalion received its orders: a reconnaissance in force on the left flank of Dumont's rebels.

The Port Hope Battalion leaped up from their positions cheering and started on a run for the cemetery and the ravine, with Col. Williams at their head. The command, "Charge" sounded along the line of the Grenadiers and the Ninetieth and they too jumped up and ran forward, firing as they went.

General Middleton watched aghast as the troops poured over the crest of the hill. "Cease firing!" he roared. Why in the name of God don't you cease firing?"

He had the bugle sound the command to retire, again and again, but the excited troopers ignored it. Within ten minutes the whole Canadian line was in motion. Middleton, at last realizing that his army was completely out of his control, called up the rear echelon troops to support the charging forward troops. From the right flank the scouts and Howard raced to the crest of the ravine and the Gatling's deadly bursts of fire was added to the rifle's continuous firing.

The Grenadiers, Midland and Ninetieth swept headlong into the first row of the Metis rifle pits. Their defenders being unable to reload quickly enough and were overcome. The excited Canadians, sensing a victory, rushed on. Some of the Metis fighters were bayoneted, one of them, dying, seized a pistol dropped by an attacking Canadian and emptied it before he was finished off. A young trooper stumbled over a body in a rifle pit and paused momentarily to stare; the Metis enemy was a dried-up old man, his hair pure white. (He was Joseph Oullette, ninety-three years old.) Dumont had ordered the elderly Oullette to withdraw from his position, the white-haired old frontiersman replied, "Wait, I want to kill another Englishman."

Dumont's Metis fighters fired the last of their bullets at the oncoming Canadians

The Metis defenders held to their pits and trenches to the last possible moment, fire their short-range weapons, then fled to the next line of defense lower on the hill, attempting to reload as they ran. Many were barefoot; during the days of cramped discomfort in the trenches may of the valiant fighters formed the habit of kicking off their leather boots or moccasins.

Col. Van Straubenzie's troops broke through the weakened Metis lines near the church, and the battle was over in minutes as the Field Force broke through the defenses, sweeping down the slope through Batoche and the now-emptied rifle pits.

As the Batoche defenders fled, some bareheaded as well as barefoot, began to feel raindrops on their faces and glanced heavenward incredulously. Powder smoke had been drifting into the ravine and they had not noticed the sky darkening. Now as they peered through rifts in the smoke they saw that the sun was now gone. A heavy overcast had brought twilight to Batoche though it was only three o'clock. This then, was the end, as Riel had foretold it; somehow they had offended, and God had withdrawn his protection of the Metis cause and their struggles. As the men stumbled down the hillside, some of the warriors sobbed.

Creeping to the mouths of their straw-littered caves in the riverbanks, the women watched the darkness fall; they moaned distractedly or sang the Cree death chants they had heard their mothers sing. In the chapel of the parish house, led by Father Fourmond, all the nuns and priests also recited the rosary together.

Foot by foot down the hillside the rebels were dislodged and driven to their trenches and pits in the meadow. Here they were able to check the Canadian's briefly, and all the firing ceased again when a messenger bearing a white flag rode from the village and on up the trail to Middleton's command position. It was Mr. Astley again bearing a new letter from Louis Riel. "General," Riel wrote, "your prompt answer to my note shows that I was correct in mentioning to you the cause of humanity. We will gather our families in one place. "But on the back of the note was a hasty hysterical scribble. I do not like war, and if you do not retreat and refuse an interview, the question remaining the same, the prisoners." Middleton ignored the note without considering its content very long and ordered Astley to remain with the troops.

The soldier's charge was resumed. Now the Metis fled from some of their positions and into their ruined houses and cabins, and fired from the windows and holes in the walls, then to the trees near the river. In this cover, their last stand on the east side of the stream, Gabriel Dumont and seven or eight others held off the foremost unit of the Canadians for about half an hour. Gabriel still had cartridges for his Winchester; some of the others were forced to use pebbles, nails, and even soft metal buttons which they shaped with their teeth.

In the Batoche House the Canadians found a pole wedged between ceiling and the floor, knocked it out and opened a trap door through which they helped eleven prisoners to emerge. They were all white-faced, haggard, nearly starved; some of them had not seen daylight in almost two months. They had been fairly well fed in the first weeks of their confinement but as food stocks in Batoche dwindled they had been put on bread and water, and for two days not even had that.

Captain French, a former Northwest Mountie and one of the leaders of the charge, leaned from a window of the Batoche House to cheer his men on, and was promptly shot dead by a Metis sniper. The militia fought its way from house to house. In the last one, Young Private Williams of the Ninetieth, the first to enter, found no living foe; but he stumbled over an open casket in which lay a pretty, young Metis girl, killed by a stray bullet or shrapnel. He judged her to be about fourteen; the body was clothed in a stiff, embroidered burial dress, white and clean. William picked up the casket and moved it to a table by the wall where it would not be upset by others who may follow him. While he was doing so, Col. Williams, hero of the charge, borrowed his rifle and began firing from a window at snipers.

Captain Ted Brown was also subsequently shot and killed by a sniper in the process of clearing Batoche. The Canadians found and freed 17 surveyors, storekeepers and settlers who Riel's Metis had captured and held in 10-foot by 12-foot hole in the ground for 18 days.

Within an hour of the start of the attack the major resistance had been crushed, but intermittent shooting continued from across the river until about seven o'clock. All their cause was now lost, some 50 to 60 Metis warriors – only 40 having rifles – were still fighting during the final minutes but they were soon overwhelmed by Middleton's troops. By seven p.m. The Canadian forces had rounded up more than 200 Metis prisoners, while their women and children had now begun to emerge from their cellars and riverbank cave shelters.

Even though the fighting had been fierce at times, casualties in the Batoche fighting were relatively light. Middleton had lost eight men killed and 46 wounded, while the Metis dead were listed at sixteen, with 30 wounded. One casualty was 10-year old Marcile Gratton, shot at one of the stores as she had tried to make a dash to her mother's hiding place. As her father and mother grieved over her body after the conflict ended, a Canadian soldier was reportedly overheard to say, "I'd sooner have let them keep Batoche than to have hurt one hair of that poor little girl."

Louis Riel and Dumont had vanished. The Canadians had moved their camp to Batoche. First the Metis women, then gradually the men, dragged into the village to give themselves up. Only a few ringleaders, Middleton assured them, would be held; but all firearms must be surrendered. Some of the men protested. They had no crops; without guns they would starve. But they acknowledged that they should have thought of that before.

The victorious troops raided the cabins and caves for souvenirs that evening, and the nuns of St. Antoine, who had been imprisoned for weeks, took the exercise they had long needed. Chattering like a flock of birds, hardly able to believe that they were mot, after all, destined to be all martyrs, the sisters walked to the army's abandoned stockade.. They marveled over the earthworks, clucked about the mess in the compound. They discovered that the troops had left some heavy kettles with hardly any holes in them, and some splendid empty barrels; these would be useful at the missions. There was also one hen, unconcerned with war and the fate of peoples, pecking at grain spilled from the horsed feed bins. The nuns were delighted. They would send faithful Baptiste with a wagon for the kettles and kegs; the hen they carried back themselves. So everyone, except the Metis, got souvenirs of the battle for Batoche.

Sightseers from the Steamer Northcote, which was remaining to evacuate the wounded, had to listen to boasting from their comrades of the land force, and had shamefully little with which to match it, but they too, were drawn to the souvenir hunt and the guided tours of the battlefield.

One of these wanderers from the Northcote strolled into the grove in which the Metis had met daily to listen to Riel's comments and prayers. He found a souvenir there but did not take it. He found nailed to a tree a cardboard placard draped in a scrap of white muslin. It was just a rough and ragged board ripped from some packing box, but affixed to it was a cheap, shiny lithograph - the Sacred Heart of Jesus. The chromo had been attached to to the card with the pointed, tiny tags used to designate the brand name on plug tobacco. The afternoon's rain, sifting through the leaves of the poplars, had done some damage; the muslin was moist and the cardboard was becoming stained and limp.

The Canadian found himself strangely moved. He would tell the others about it: he had found a cardboard shrine. He went away then, back to ruined Batoche, to the cardboard capitol of the new nation, whence two hundred men in mounted patrols had been sent out to find Riel and Dumont. If he shared the opinions of his fellows, he reflected that one of whom that the troops sought to find so eagerly, one was only a cardboard prophet, the other a fighting man, was solid oak. It would not have mattered if the Canadians had removed the picture from the grove, for the shrine would never be used again. The beaten Metis, miserable and unbelieving, now began to shuffle up the hill in long, silent lines hoping to seek comfort in the church.

Father Vegreville welcomed his prodigal flock; the priests had long been agreed that it was all Riel's fault. He helped them bury the dead - in a mass grave except for "old one" Joseph Oulette, for whom Father Fourmond had somehow provided a newly-hewed coffin; they could not have the full rites of the Catholic Church, but there were suitable prayers by their grieving families.

Father Vegreville was generous with the small quantity of food he had been able to obtain from mission stores in the district, and he intervened vigorously with Middleton to get Government relief. But the priest was overzealous. He also agreed to act as the Government's commissioner, to receive the submission of the rebels and to collect their guns. He found about a hundred weapons; nearly all the rest had been previously surrendered to the troops.

The Metis when necessary could worship at a cardboard shrine, confess each other, and offer their simple prayers directly to their God. Penitent they might be, but they were not yet wholly without spirit, and they did not fancy their priest in the role of agent for their conquerors. A few weeks later, his usefulness at an end, Father Vegreville left the district. Swiftly now the spiritual and temporal power of the church crumbled. The Metis, destitute and disillusioned, neglected their religious duties and withdrew their children from the parochial school. The young people gave themselves up to dissipation and mocked the priests. Father Fourmond's once prosperous mission of St. Laurent failed and for a time was abandoned. Diocesan headquarters were moved to Prince Albert. The little church of St. Antoine at Batoche, however survived and still functions. "For a while," Father Fourmond wrote, "we had hoped to regain the confidence of the Metis; like our Lord, we can but repeat his words: How often have I wanted to gather thee, as the hen doth gather the chickens under her wings, and thou wouldst not."

Chapter 12
THE TRIAL: HERO OR TRAITOR

The day after the brave defenders of their village – and their decades old way of life – succumbed to vastly superior Dominion forces, Louis Riel surrendered to a mounted party of Canadian scouts and taken to Regina to stand trial for treason. Gabriel Dumont managed to elude his pursuers and escape to the United States. His superior marksmanship with his trusty Winchester enabled the Metis Prince of the Prairies to appear in Buffalo Bill's Wild West Show and display his shooting ability for a period. Years later Dumont was pardoned and resumed his former life as a hunter. The rest of the provisional government was caught and also charged with treason and other crimes against the Government of Canada. The other Metis leaders were either imprisoned or, like Dumont, disappeared until a general amnesty was proclaimed. Any of the Metis fighters who had not escaped were held for later judgment.

Louis Riel was quickly taken by steamboat to Saskatoon, thence in a heavily-guarded wagon caravan to Moose Jaw, and from there by special train to Regina, where the Government had ordered him to be incarcerated. The Saskatchewan Territorial capitol had no prison except the guardhouse of the Northwest Mounted Police headquarters, so Riel was put there to await trial.

In the evening of that first day of his imprisonment Louis was nervous. Mindful of the persecutions he had suffered fifteen years before – the threats to kill him, the warrant for his arrest, his exile to Montana – he feared an outbreak of violence among the troops directed at him.

But the orderly Canadians who had gathered to view their opponent when he was allowed to leave his tent, under heavy-guard, were respectful rather than displaying any anger or resentment toward Riel. They would stare at him, but to Riel's astonishment he was not even reviled or insulted as he passed among the men. General Middleton and his staff treated him as a gentleman, an equal, and, after a few days, almost in a friendly manner. Louis, a beaten half-breed, being treated so cordially by the Canadians was pathetically grateful for this consideration.

During the evening of the first day, General Middleton ordered a tent set up beside his own tent. This was to be Riel's prison until word came from Ottawa as to what was to be done with him. Captain George H. Young of the general staff was ordered to remain with Riel day and night, and sentries constantly patrolled the tent, but Louis was not manacled or chained.

Captain Young, a Winnipeg man, had known Louis in 1870; he was the son of the Methodist preacher who had comforted Thomas Scott in his last hour at Fort Garry. He and Riel talked frequently, but with one or two exceptions, and then only under orders. Young did not attempt to extract information the prisoner did not want to divulge. When such questions would occasionally arise, Young found Riel to be a master of deception.

Captain Young and Riel spent eight days together. When they parted, Louis had acquired considerable affection for his jailor, and Young acknowledged profound respect for Riel.

Young later admitted that during their discussions that Louis Riel was "better educated and much more clever than I was." In one sense, Young's high opinion of Riel's intellect turned out to be unfortunate; it was impossible for him to conceive that this man who had bested him in arguments might be mad, therefore his later testimony helped to send Riel to the gallows.

During their many discussions Riel tried to explain that there had been no hope of defeating Canada or Great Britain; they had planned only to make a stand, to show strength sufficient to convince the Dominion that it must negotiate honorably with the neglected people of the Northwest Territories – including the white settlers of Prince Albert who had encouraged the movement until they were needed to support the Metis.

The records of the Metis council recovered after Batoche, General Middleton told him had been impounded. Louis was glad; he felt that the papers would prove that he had not fomented the rebellion, that leadership had been thrust upon him, that he had not wanted the resultant bloodshed. But, Riel had forgotten the damning note to the Mounties Major Crozier before Duck Lake, in his hand and bearing his signature, which had threatened "To commence now and without any delay, a war of extermination."

On July 6, 1885, the charge of high treason was proposed against Louis Riel. The trial to be set before Hugh Richardson, Magistrate of the Northwest Territories, was scheduled for July 20 to be held in Regina. High treason is modern society's most grievous crime; under British law the only penalty upon conviction is death.

Riel was the only rebellion culprit to face this charge; about seventy had been indicted, but when tried, were accused of a lesser crime of treason-felony, which was not a capital offense. There can be little question that the circumstances of Louis Riel's trial were immoral. Whether the trial itself was also illegal has been debated ever since it was held.

The magistrate involved was permitted to work with a jury of only six. This was a reasonable provision in most cases because of the sparse population of settlements of the Territories, but Riel's council contended that the right of jury trial as won by the Magna Charta and later defined in statutes meant trial before a full jury of twelve.

Louis Riel's fate nevertheless was given in the hands of only six men. All were Protestants of Anglo-Saxon stock; whereas the defendant was Catholic and French. Moreover all the jurors were unfamiliar with the French language, which Riel and some of the witnesses spoke, thus being dependent upon translators for much important testimony. Riel himself, in his two speeches, used English, but the necessity of doing so put him at some disadvantage.

Justice Richardson was no stranger to the problems of the region, and also fully aware of the historical significance of his present assignment. The defense overlooked, or chose to ignore, a letter he had written in 1880 to the Interior Ministry. His letter urged prompt dealings with the many Metis grievances because the half-breed colonies had been "subjected to evil influences of leading spirits of the Manitoba problems. This characterization of Metis leadership as evil and up to no good should have cast doubts upon the fitness to judge the man the Metis regarded as their greatest, most inspirational leader of them all.

Yet Richardson's conduct of the trial, at least up to when he gave his charge to the jury, was above reproach. His charge, while perhaps legally sound, was definitely prejudicial, and the wording of the sentence would seem to have been unnecessarily cruel.

The charging information contained six counts listing three overt acts – levying war against the Crown at Duck Lake, Fish Creek and Batoche. In counts one, two and three, Riel was described as a subject of our Lady the Queen. In counts four, five and six he was said to be merely "living within the Dominion of Canada and under the" protection of the Queen. Riel, having acquired United States citizenship while exiled in Montana, was not a subject of the Queen and could not be guilty of violating his "natural allegiance."

During his trial Riel gave two lengthy speeches that demonstrated his powerful, fluent, and rhetorical abilities. Even though his counselors advised, Riel rejected their attempts to prove he was not guilty by reason of insanity.

Hours later, as the trial wound down, "Gentlemen," the clerk asked, "are you agreed upon your verdict? How say you – is the prisoner guilty or not guilty?" Jury foremen, Cosgrave, a gentlemanly middle-aged Englishmen, did not look at the defendant; his grave gaze was fixed upon Judge Richardson. His voice was low and clear. "We find the defendant guilty" he said. Riel swayed momentarily, leaning against the railing. "Gentlemen of the jury" the clerk said, "hearken to your verdict as the court records it: you find the prisoner, Louis Riel guilty, so say you all." "Guilty," they murmured.

"Your Honor," Cosgrave addressed Richardson, "I have been

asked by my brother jurors to recommend the defendant, Louis Riel, to the mercy of the Crown." Judge Richardson replied, that "the recommendation you have given will be forwarded to the proper authorities."

"Louis Riel," Richardson asked, "Have you anything to say why the sentence of the court should not be pronounced upon you, for the offense of which you have been found guilty?" Riel stared into the judge's face. There was a pause before he spoke. "Yes – your Honor - "he continued, "Your Honor, gentlemen of the jury, (Until then, Louis said, he had been considered insane, or criminal or just someone to be shunned.) "I suppose that after being condemned I will cease to be called a fool, and for me it is an advantage. If I have a mission – I say 'if' for the sake of those who doubt, but for my part it means 'since' since I have a mission, I cannot fulfill my mission as long as I am looked upon as an insane being. Should I be executed, I would not be executed as an insane man. It would be a great consolation for my mother, my wife, for my relatives, for my countrymen."

After listening patiently, Judge Richardson addressed Riel, "You have been found guilty of treason and the court recommends that you shall be taken to the place of execution and hanged by the neck until you are dead."

Riel still stood at his place, bracing himself. No one could discern a change of expression when the sentence was pronounced, but his body had slumped. Among the onlookers the sentence caused an obvious sense of excitement, even some shock and disbelief.

The date of Riel's execution was set for November 16, 1885. Perhaps the most controversial figure in Canadian history, Louis Riel led a life that has spawned a massive and diverse literature.

It is ironic that after so many years of considering him a traitor, the Canadian Government may soon posthumously pardon Riel and perhaps even officially name him as one of the fathers of the Confederation. Gabriel Dumont had become a folk hero and is commemorated, among other means, by a provincial educational institution wholly owned and controlled by the Metis Nation of

Saskatchewan Province. After the rebellion and furor over Riel's hanging, the Metis People have made significant strides in their decades-long struggle to be recognized as a distinct people, with land, economic and social rights similar to those gained by native counterparts.

As the fateful November day arrived, the Regina area population began to take a great interest in the manner that Riel would face death. The precautions taken against a jail delivery, supposed to be secret, were soon common knowledge and added to the overall excitement.

The gallows had been erected in a fenced enclosure adjoining the guardroom where Riel was confined. The platform, concealed by the fence, had been placed so that the only access to it was through an upstairs window, which was barred. On November 15, the barracks blacksmith, Sergeant Robinson, cut the bars away.

That night Riel wrote his last letter to his mother and a few other notes. He spent most of the night in prayer with the priest; he was calm and showed no fear. At five o'clock in the morning, Father Andre said Mass and administered his last communion.

The morning was cold and clear. At dawn the people began to assemble in the field before the barracks square. A strong cordon of barrack's Mounties had been drawn up around the enclosure and no one without a pass could gain entrance. At eight-fifteen Deputy Sheriff Gibson appeared at the door of Riel's cell. The French-Canadian sheriff, S.E. Chapleau, usually in charge, attended the execution, but took no part in it. Riel was talking easily with Father Andre when the deputy appeared. Riel looked up, "You want me, Mr. Gibson?" he asked. "I am ready."

Riel and father Andre walked into the corridor, where they were joined by other officials and another priest, Father McWilliams, who had been sent by Toronto sympathizers to offer help to Riel during his last trying moments. Riel face was set and he moved slowly. He was hatless and his heavy brown hair was shiny from the brushing he had given it. He wore a short, black jacket, dark brown trousers and moccasins. He held a silver-mounted ivory crucifix which he kissed as he prayed. To Father

Andre he said that he forgave his enemies, offered his life as a sacrifice to God, and repented his sins. The two priests placed their hands on his head and pronounced the ablution.

Riel's arms were then pinioned be the guards, they stooped and passed through the window onto a small ledge above the gallows platform. He looked over the fence to the people milling about, to the prairie: It was glistering in the sun, the air crisp and cool; the kind of a morning any Metis loved, a morning on which to start a trip. He went down the few steps to the gallows platform, gently maneuvered by the guards to a position on the trap. His face was dead white, beaded with perspiration.

Father Andre followed along behind. Riel glanced at him. *"Courage, mon pere,"* he said. The priests and Dr. Jukes shook hands with him. The hangman came forward and slipped the noose over his head. "I should like to pray a little more," Riel asked. "Two minutes", Gibson said. "Say 'Our Father'", Father Mc-Williams suggested to Riel, then turned to Gibson and whispered an aside: "When he comes to 'deliver us from evil,' tell him then." He nodded toward the hangman. Gibson motioned for the hangman to come forward and instructed him in a whisper.

The hangman moved beside Riel, dropping a white cotton hood over his head. Fumbling with the rope, he brought his lips closer to Riel's ear. "Louis Riel," he said in a hoarse, angry whisper, "Do you know me? You cannot escape from me today!" Louis stood firmly erect. The hood concealed whatever indignity he may have felt – one incredible, final indignity to be killed by a man who bore him a personal grudge.

The executioner had waited a long time for his revenge. He was Jack Henderson, who claimed to have been a prisoner of Riel at Fort Garry in 1870 with his friend Thomas Scott who was executed at that time after Riel's council's verdict of death. He had told Riel then, he boasted, "I'll be the man to put the hangman's knot under your ear." Father McWilliams led the last prayer in English. Riel's voice was fainter now but still clear. "Our Father who art...lead us not into temptation, but deliver us - "The trap opened and Riel's body plunged down nine feet. It quivered and swayed on the taut rope. Thus ended a man's dream and prayers for a new, glorious destiny for his beloved Metis people.

A narrow interpretation of the Metis leader's legacy is that he was either a hero or villain for defending the indigenous rights through armed rebellion. In 1869 the conclusion in many grade ten history classes seems to be that he Riel was simultaneously right and, wrong for resisting government annexation of his people's homeland.

The Metis National Council President, Clement Chartier says the Metis peoples are at the very core of what it means to be Canadian. The Metis language, Michif, is a blend of French, Ojibwa, Cree and Assiniboine. Their ancestral lands stretch from Manitoba to Alberta and the Northwest Territories. The Metis people were the most prolific fur traders of colonial North America, establishing settlements and trading posts deep within Canada's vast wilderness. Most importantly, Chartier said, the Metis-led Red River rebellion of 1869 resulted in the creation of Canada's first prairie province. Because the Metis resisted in having their land annexed – and, in so doing formed a provisional government that negotiated Manitoba's entry into Canada – the Government was able to secure the completion of its most crucial nation-building project: the intercontinental railroad spanning the Nation.

Despite the Metis historic importance within Canada, the Federal Government almost immediately embarked on a campaign to assimilate and suppress them following the rebellion and, subsequent creation of Manitoba. The 1879 Manitoba Act guaranteed a land grant of 1.4 million acres to the Metis, but less than half of the territory was ever ceded.

For Canada's 150th birthday, some politicians and activists have demanded the Conservatives pardon Louis Riel. However that didn't interest Chartier. "A pardon implies that Riel performed something wrong and he is being forgiven," he said. "We believe that he did no wrong. We want to get the things that Riel fought and died for: land base and self-government.... our preference is, as one of our Metis professors says, 'let the stain remain' .It's not a stain on us, it's a stain on Canada and how they treated the Metis peoples."

Riel's hanging created a furor in Quebec. The Quebec ministers in Macdonald's cabinet had given out hints that Riel would have his death sentence commuted. The newspapers tried to pressure Macdonald to step in, but Macdonald was not going to be pressured. Macdonald claimed that he would have hanged anyone who did what Riel had done, whatever his name, whatever his ethnic origin. John Thompson of Nova Scotia, Macdonald's new Minister of Justice, explained to Parliament that anyone who raised the Indian's to war could not expect to get off with punishment less than that which the Indians themselves received.

James W. Taylor wrote to the United States State Department on November 3[rd,]"The impression prevails that there will be no further respite of the execution of Louis Riel." Now Taylor made his last appeal. The Dominion, he contended, had violated his pledge to the Metis in 1870, a pledge which had won its permission from the United States to transport some of Wolesley's supplies south of the boundary. He urged immediate intervention to save Riel while the whole problem of U. S. -Canadian relations in the Northwest was studied. But the State Department was unmoved by Taylor's pleas, or by petitions received from a growing number of French-Canadian communities.

The last hope in Washington rested with a faithful friend of the doomed man – Edmond Mallet. He obtained an interview with Secretary of State Thomas Bayard, but Bayard told him the United States would not intervene. Mallet finally was received by President Cleveland, making an eloquent plea on political and moral grounds: Riel was an American citizen, unfairly tried; he was insane. .President Cleveland told Mallet he was much interested, but late that night the Associated Press office in Washington told Mallet "the President has been constrained to decline interfering."

Today, 128 years later, the Northwest rebellion still sparks opposite opinions. Was Louis Riel a hero or a traitor? To the Canadian Government in Ottawa at the time he was thought of and represented as a "Benedict Arnold", a traitor to his country by fomenting an armed revolt of the Metis. Many other Canadians, especially the Metis peoples in the Northwest Saskatchewan territory consider Riel a patriot, a la "Nathan Hale" - "Give me liberty or give me death."

Today many streets, schools and other facilities in Metis populated areas are named after Riel. Additionally the Government in Ottawa has been petitioned to pardon Riel in absentia.

But there still remained Gabriel Dumont. He and Michel Dumas had crossed the Montana line about June 1st and had given themselves up to United States troops at Fort Assiniboine, just south of the boundary. The commanding officer of that remote Montana post wired Washington for instructions. President Cleveland, declaring them to be political refugees and thus entitled to a haven in the U.S., ordered them released.

Dumont hastened to Spring Lake, the most prosperous Metis colony, and set to work to plan the escape of Riel. He visited other settlements, collected money, horses and men, and by October he was ready. At intervals of every ten to twenty miles from Lewistown, Montana to Regina, Saskatchewan, four hundred and fifty miles, he established secret relay stations with fresh mounts, armed men for escorts, and food for the fugitive. Every Metis and Indian camp had been alerted; if Riel had reached any one of them he would have vanished forever from the White man's world. Gabriel Dumont, without ever knowing it recreated the under-ground railway of the Civil War.

Sadly, his efforts went for naught in November as Louis Riel's dreams of an Independent, self-governing Metis Nation, along with Gabriel Dumont's brilliant military tactics failed.

ADDENDUM

Though an American living in California, I found the 1885 Metis rebellion extremely intriguing even though in scope, participants, casualties and impact upon a nation rather nominal compared to the American Revolution 25 years earlier.

To me the most compelling and interesting aspect of the rebellion concerns their leader and spokesman, Louis Riel. A bigger than life personality; his struggle to not only to represent his peoples' needs and interests with a rather un- sympathetic Dominion Government in Ottawa, but to encourage and lead them to achieve his dream of a self-governing, God-fearing independent nation. Indeed, free from the burgeoning incursions into their decades-old territories and way of life by ever-increasing inroads of white settlers.

The outcome of the rebellion – especially the hanging of Louis Riel, actually engendered feelings of sadness and regret. Especially in that Riel was somewhat a "Nathan Hale" figure - "Give me liberty or give me death" rather than a murderous, tyrannical leader such as Fidel Castro, Mao, Pol Pot, etc.

In this regard, during the rebellion he never fired a shot but exhorted his Metis people by riding among them praying and waving a foot-and-a-half long crucifix. In addition, as a testament to his inherent humanity, at the conclusion of the Duck Lake and Fish Creek battles he prevented Gabriel Dumont, his military commander, from pursuing retreating Canadian forces and annihilating them. Riel chastened Dumont in both instances saying, "There's been enough bloodshed already – let them go." Unfortunately these humane acts weren't brought up by Riel's defense during his trial.

As an interesting aside, during Hollywood's 'Golden Age', a movie was made depicting the Metis rebellion. I say 'depicted' grudgingly as it was a very loose, fact-flawed version. The movie was in Technicolor featuring the Canadian Northwest Mounted (eventually to become designated as the Royal Canadian Mounted Police) in their glamorous, scarlet-red Norfolk tunics.

The featured actors we'll all remember fondly I'm sure: Gary Cooper, Paulette Goddard, Preston Foster, Madeleine Carrol, Robert Preston and Akim Tamiroff.

As an example of flawed facts – decidedly important – was the deadly Gatling gun, the forerunner to machine guns. In the movie the Gatling gun was portrayed using deadly effect by the Metis, when in actuality the opposite was true; the Canadian government forces had the use of the Gatling, and its use was crucial in the final engagement in Riel's last stand at the Batoche battle.

CANADIAN HIGHLITES

Canada is 2nd largest nation in the world.

Greatest asset: natural resources; (fishing, timber, farming, hydro-electric power, petroleum, iron ore, and other minerals)

Officially a bilingual nation.

Most Canadians live within 100 miles of U.S. Border.

Canada is big! It spans six times zones; covering 3.8 million square miles; ten provinces and three territories.

Canada holds about two million lakes, the largest being Great Bear Lake.

Canada's wildlife: Beaver, Mink, Muskrat, Moose, Deer, Bighorn sheep, Polar bears, and many others

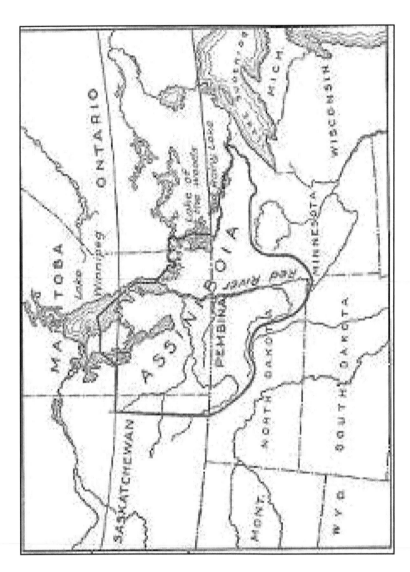

ASSINIBOIA NATION Strange Empire/Howard.

GLOSSARY

TIMELINE

A.D. 1002: Leif Erikson reaches Baffin Island on the coast of Newfoundland.

1497: John Cabot lands on Canada's eastern coast, claims region for England.

1535: Jacques Cartier claims the land at two Indian villages for France. The two villages would later become Montreal and Quebec.

1610: English explorer Henry Hudson discovers the Hudson Bay.

1615: French missionaries arrive to convert Indians to Christianity.

1627: England and France go to war in Europe and in North America.

1763: The Treaty of Paris signed, ceding all French territories in what was to become Canada to the British.

1774: Britain passes the Quebec Act, giving the French Canadian population religious liberty and the right to follow its own laws.

1784: New Brunswick is established off the east coast.

1791: The Constitutional Act splits Quebec into upper and lower Canada.

1837: Revolts occur in both upper and lower Canada.

1841: The Union Act joins upper and lower Canada, becoming the Province of Canada.

1867: The North America Act forms the Dominion of Canada by the English.

1870-73: Canada acquires Manitoba, the Northwest Territories, British Columbia and Prince Edward Island.

1885: Louis Riel leads the Northwest rebellion of Metis - the only armed rebellion in Canadian history.

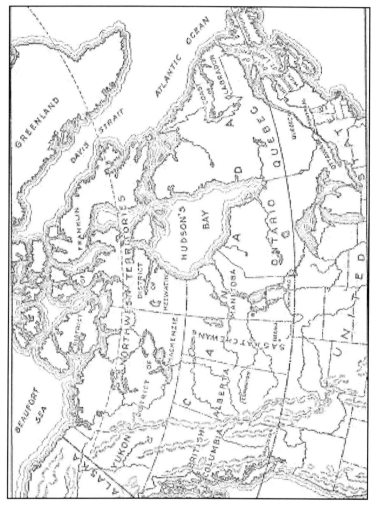

Canadian provinces. Strange Empire/Howard.

Country: Canada

Area: 3.8 million sq. miles

Land Areas:
St. Lawrence, Appalachian, Canadian Shield, Interior Prairie, Cordilleran, Arctic.

Major Rivers: St. Lawrence, Columbia, Mackenzie, Yukon, Fraser, Churchill

Wildlife: Beavers, mink, muskrat, moose, deer, bighorn sheep, bears, seals, walrus, caribou, polar bears, ducks, geese, trout, perch, bass, whitefish, pike, salmon, halibut, cod, mackerel, haddock, herring

Capital City: Ottawa

Major Cities: Montreal, Vancouver, Toronto

Languages: English and French

Monetary: Canadian dollar

Canadian Currency: One dollar Canadian = 100 cents.
The Bank of Canada is the official bank of Canada and prints the legal notes. The Bank prints notes in $5 - $10 -$20 - $50- $100 – and $1,000 denominations. The $1 note was replaced by a coin in 1989, and the $2 note was replaced by coin in 1996. The Canadian coin is designed, minted and distributed by the Royal Canadian Mint. Coins are minted in the denominations of 1c- 5c - 10c- 25c- 50c- $1, and $2.

Illustrations

Indian Nations 1800
Dominion of Canada 1870
Pembina, Ft. Garry area
Louis Riel age 39
Conflict area 1885
Assiniboia Nation
Canadian provinces